Margaret Picton

Understanding Homemaking

Illustrated by Doreen Lang

Blackie

BLACKIE & SON LTD
Bishopbriggs · Glasgow G64 2NZ
•
450/452 Edgware Road · London W2 1EG

First Published 1976
ISBN 0 216 90125 1

TO COLIN, KERRY AND BRYONE

Filmset in Plantin by
Filmtype Services Ltd, Scarborough
Printed in Great Britain by
Thomson Litho Ltd, East Kilbride

Contents

Part One

Choosing a Home

What is a home?

Why do we live in buildings? You may be able to think of many reasons for being glad that you have a roof over your head at night and a particular place you can call your own. Imagine what it would be like to have nowhere to go. What would you do during the winter? How would you keep warm and dry?

Houses provide us with ***shelter*** from the weather and give us a feeling of ***warmth*** and ***security***.

During the Stone Age, primitive man lived in caves or in rough shelters made from rocks and the branches of trees. When he learned to make simple tools, such as the hand-axe, he was able to build stronger shelters for his family. These early buildings were the first homes. In the Stone Age, houses were necessary for protection from the wild animals that roamed the countryside. The buildings we think of today as homes are far more elaborate than the simple Stone Age shelters, but we need our houses for the very same reasons that our ancestors needed their shelters.

When is a house a home?

Have you ever stopped to ask yourself the question, "What is the difference between a house and a home?" A ***house***, as we have already said, provides people with shelter but a ***home*** provides people with far more than this. A home is where a family lives. A home is a place where there is love and understanding. There may also be quarrels and angry scenes, because these are part of family life and of learning to live together, but through all these difficulties the members of a family will be loyal to each other. In a home, each member is important and is loved for what he or she is like, for the bad points as well as the good ones. This is what makes a house into a home.

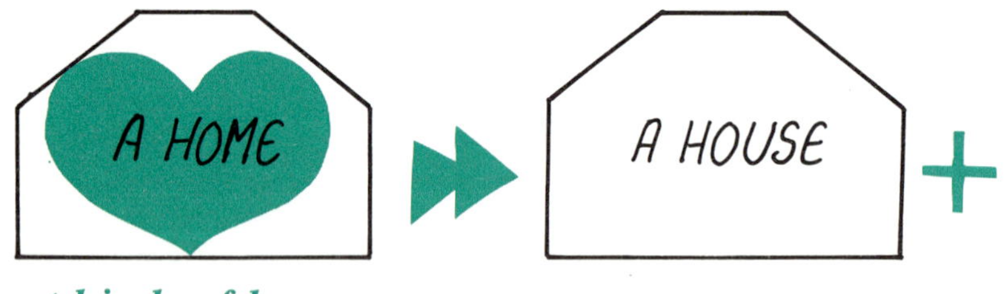

Different kinds of homes

Any building can be turned into a home, but if a building has a good water supply and drainage, good sanitary arrangements and plenty of light, heat and space, it becomes a far healthier place in which to live. For these reasons most young married couples choose to live in houses, flats or caravans.

1 Houses

At the beginning of this century, houses were often built in long terraces. They did not have gardens and the toilets, sometimes communal (shared with other houses), were in the back yard. These terraced houses were economical to build but were dark, cramped and inconvenient places to live. Today, houses are designed with more care and thought. They usually have a garden, with space for a garage if necessary, and have plenty of light, space and modern equipment. Houses can be ***detached***, ***semi-detached*** or built in small groups as ***terraced town*** houses.

A detached house usually requires more land than a semi-detached or terraced house does, so it is more expensive to buy or rent, but it does have plenty of garden space for recreation or cultivation and this also gives more privacy. A semi-detached house is more economical with land, but still has ample garden and garage space. It is therefore less expensive to buy or rent than a detached house, and for this reason is popular with young married couples. A terraced town house is found in heavily populated areas of towns and cities, where building land is very expensive and often difficult to find. The modern town house usually has some garden space, though this may be small. The interior design is well planned.

Bungalows, both detached and semi-detached, are usually built with one storey only and are popular with older people who dislike or have difficulty in climbing stairs.

2 *Flats*

Many large, old houses are converted into small flats or bedsitters. These units can then become economical homes for single people or for married couples who cannot afford the expense of buying or renting a complete house. Flats, such as these, can be self-contained or they can have shared washing, cooking and toilet facilities. Obviously, a self-contained flat is to be preferred to a communal arrangement, because of the practical and health problems involved in the sharing of kitchens and bathrooms. If the rented accommodation is not self-contained, both landlord and tenant must respect each other's privacy, belongings and way of life.

Some local authorities favour the building of blocks of modern, self-contained flats, because of the shortage of building land. For many families, these flats are the answer to their housing problem. They are relatively inexpensive to buy or rent but they do have some disadvantages, especially for couples with young families. There is often very little playspace for young children. The concrete, communal playgrounds sometimes provided do not compare with the privacy and comparative safety of house gardens. There are often practical problems to be considered too, such as the parking of prams and the negotiating of stairs or lifts, especially in high-rise flats. There may also be medical problems arising from feelings of insecurity and isolation that some families experience in high-rise flats. The most popular flats have only five or six floors.

3 Caravans

A caravan is home to many families. A caravan can be rented or bought but it must be remembered that it cannot be parked just anywhere. Some residential sites are available for caravan families. These sites provide the necessary toilet facilities and some are even equipped with shops and a launderette, but the plot of land needed for each caravan must be rented or bought. Caravans vary in size but many are large and well-equipped internally. Obviously, caravans are not as spacious as houses, and for a family, storage space and privacy can pose problems. There is not the same freedom of movement for children, who can feel very confined. With young children in bed early, adults are also very restricted in what they can do.

It is sometimes impossible for a newly-married couple to afford one of these kinds of homes and while they are saving for a home of their own, they may choose to live with parents. This arrangement is not usually good and can lead to unhappiness and quarrels within a family. A newly-married couple need privacy and a chance to get to know each other, and these are often lacking in such a situation. If living with parents is necessary for a while, an attempt should be made to give the young couple one room which they can call their own. A small bedroom can be turned into a homely bedsitting room, with just a little thought and care, and though meals may be shared with the rest of the family, the young couple will have some privacy and a place of their own when they need it.

The type of home chosen will depend upon many factors. The amount of money available, the nearness to a place of work, the size and age of the family will all have to be considered. It should be remembered that however simple or luxurious the surrounding shell may be, a home is created by the love and understanding of the people who live there.

Think and Do

1. Prepare a class frieze on "Houses through the ages".
2. List the advantages and disadvantages of living in a block of high-rise flats, for a young couple with children.
3. Write a poem entitled "Home".
4. From magazines, collect pictures of as many different kinds of homes as you can find. Stick them into your note-book and underneath each picture write some advantages and disadvantages of living in each one.
5. Use the school and local libraries to find out the meaning of the following terms:
a. high-rise flats;
b. town houses;
c. new town developments;
d. communal facilities;
e. bedsitters;
f. self-contained flats.
6. Read the words of the folk song "Home Sweet Home". Can you think of a modern version of this song?

7. Copy the following diagram into your notebook and write a suitable sentence in each of the boxes.

8. How would you try to turn a house into a home for your family?

9. Look at the property section in your local newspaper. Read some of the advertisements of property for sale.

a. Imagine you are wanting to buy a small, modern flat. List the points you would look for when choosing a property.

b. Imagine you are trying to sell a 3-bedroomed semi-detached house. Make up a suitable advertisement giving as many details as you think fit.

10. Make a model of a house using an empty cereal box. Decorate the model as attractively as you can. You may wish to use glue, paint, varnish or gummed paper.

Buying or renting a home

When you have decided where you would like to live and in what type of building, then you can start looking around for suitable properties. The money you have available will govern whether you can ***buy*** a property or whether you will have to ***rent*** one.

Buying a property

A person who buys a house, flat or caravan, and then lives in it, is called the ***owner occupier***. It is not often that a person has enough money to pay for a property outright. Money can be borrowed from several sources:

- ***a*** building societies;
- ***b*** banks;
- ***c*** insurance companies;
- ***d*** local authorities.

The state of the country's finances will affect how easy it is to borrow money at any particular time. The person who lends the money will need to know that the person wanting a loan has a regular income (wage or salary) and will be able to repay the loan.

When money is borrowed in order to buy a property, it is called a ***mortgage***. A person applying for a mortgage will agree to repay the money borrowed plus interest, in regular amounts over a period of years. Interest is the profit required by the lender and this may fluctuate (go up or down) periodically. The deeds or title documents of the property are held by the lender until the payments are completed. Mortgages are usually repaid after 20 to 25 years but some can be obtained for longer periods.

An owner occupier has many extra expenses to budget for, in addition to his mortgage repayments.

1 General rates

This is the name given to a sum of money paid to the local authority or regional council in which the property is situated. This money will go towards local expenses such as the collection of refuse, street lighting, recreational amenities, and road works. Another part of the general rates will go towards the cost of housing, libraries, education, the social services, the police force, etc. Each property has a ***rateable value***, which is assessed (worked out) by the local valuation authority. The size of the property, the number of rooms, the total ground area, etc. are all considered when the rateable value is fixed. The rate to be paid in the pound is also decided by the local authority. The rates paid can be worked out by multiplying the rateable value by the rate in the pound.

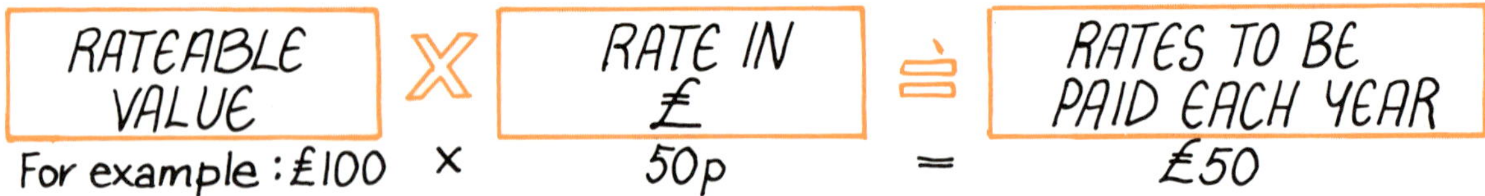

Rates can be paid annually or in instalments. There is also a charge by the regional water board for water supplies, sewerage disposal facilities and land drainage. This is known as the water rate and is also calculated on the rateable value of the property. The water rate is usually included in the general rates demand.

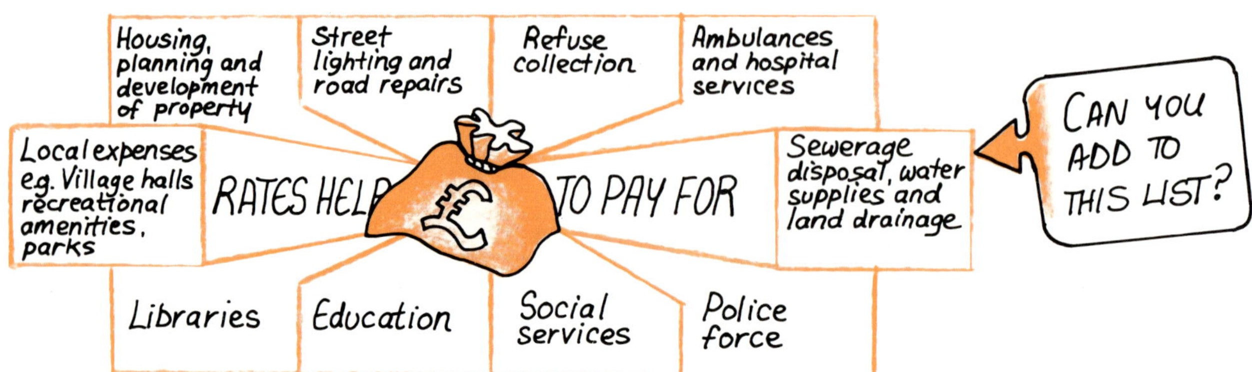

2 Insurance

When a mortgage is granted, the lender will insist on the shell of the property being insured. It is also wise, in addition, to insure the contents of the property against damage by theft, fire, water and other possible risks. This can be done by taking out an insurance policy and paying a premium to an insurance company. The premiums can be paid weekly, monthly or annually.

3 Maintenance of the property

An owner occupier is completely responsible for his property. He will have to budget to cover expenses, such as decoration and repair work, when necessary. If he is within a building where there are other residents, he will be responsible for a part share in the upkeep of such things as roofs, chimneys, etc.

4 Ground rents

Some property is bought absolutely. This means that the ground as well as the building has been bought. This is called ***freehold*** property. Some property is bought on a "lease" and a ground rent is paid half yearly or annually, to the owner of the land. This rent is in addition to the mortgage repayments. This type of property is called ***leasehold*** property. Many leases run for 999 years but some are for shorter periods. When the lease expires (runs out), the building becomes the property of the owner of the land. It is always wise, therefore, to check on the length of lease that is left before buying a leasehold property. In Scotland this ground rent is known as ***feu duty*** and it is possible to free oneself from it by paying a lump sum.

An owner occupier must budget each year for:

Renting a property

It may be advisable to consider renting rather than buying a property, if there is not enough money available to put down a deposit and not sufficient income to keep up mortgage repayments. It is also better to rent rather than buy, if the period of stay in any one place is limited.

A person who pays rent for the property in which he lives, is called the ***tenant*** and the person who owns the property is called the ***landlord***. Rent can be paid weekly, monthly or at longer intervals, and is usually collected by a rent collector or by the landlord himself.

A property can be rented ***furnished*** or ***unfurnished***. The rent is higher for a furnished house or flat than for a similar unfurnished one, because the tenant is paying for the use of the landlord's furniture. Unfurnished property is more secure but with furnished property it is easier for a landlord to put a tenant out. Property can be rented for short terms or for longer periods.

It is advisable for a person looking for rented accommodation to check with the landlord about the various expenses paid by each party, because these can vary. For very short tenancies it is usual for the landlord to pay the rates and to be responsible for the decoration and repair of the property. For longer tenancies the tenant is expected to pay the rates in addition to the rent, and also to be responsible for decorating the inside of the property. It is best therefore to have a written tenancy agreement when renting a property. This should state the amount of rent to be paid, when it is due and which other bills the tenant is to pay, e.g. for gas or electricity. There may be an extra charge for the cleaning, lighting and heating of any joint areas such as staircases, entrance halls and lifts.

Council houses and flats

A council house or flat is one that is owned by the local authority. A family which does not want to buy a property of its own, can apply to rent a council property. There is usually a waiting list for council houses and flats, and councils have to select their tenants on a "points" scheme, usually giving preference to couples with young children.

A rent is paid by the tenant to the local authority, usually through a rent collector. In some cases, rent and rates are paid together. The local authority is responsible for any repair work necessary, including the decoration of the outside of the property. The tenant is expected to decorate the inside and to keep the property clean.

Some local authorities run schemes which allow their tenants to buy the property in which they are living, if they wish.

Tied property

A tied property is one that can be rented if the tenant is employed by the landlord of the property. For example, a farm labourer may pay rent for a farm cottage, but he is only allowed to live there because he works on the farm. The cottage is "tied" to the farm and is only let to farm workers. Many large industrial firms have properties which they let in a similar way to their own workers. These tied properties can usually be rented after a worker has retired, but if the tenant moves to a different job of work and ceases to work for the landlord of the property, then he must find other accommodation.

A word about rebates

A rebate is a deduction or discount. Many people with low incomes are entitled to claim rebates on their rates. Ask at your local council offices for details of these rebate schemes and any allowances. Rate rebates can be claimed by owner occupiers and by tenants whose rates are included in their rent.

Looking at property

It is not always possible to live exactly where you would like. People wishing to live in council houses or flats, for example, have to take the right-sized accommodation, as it becomes available, and cannot always pick and choose the neighbourhood of their home. Similarly, it is not always possible for people wishing to rent property to find exactly the kind of property they want, in the right area, and their choice may be limited. It is people wishing to buy property who have the chance to "shop around" until they are satisfied.

When looking for a future home, ask yourselves the following questions. The answers will help you to decide whether the property is really what you want.

1 Can we afford the mortgage repayments/rent, rates and other expenses, and still be able to live comfortably?

2 Do we like the property?

3 Is it the right size? If the size of your family means that three bedrooms are essential, then it is a waste of time looking at two-bedroomed properties.

4 Is it convenient for work? It would be wise to check on transport services, if you do not have a car.

5 Is it near enough to shops, schools, parks, clinics, libraries? Some of these will be important to you.

6 Is the property in good condition? Beware of damp patches on walls, woodwork that looks rotten, and rooms that have a musty smell. These are bad signs and can indicate that the property has been neglected.

7 Has it got a good aspect and view? It is better to have a pleasant outlook from your windows than to be staring at a factory wall or gasworks.

8 Is the property connected to the main services, e.g. sewerage, telephone, etc.?

You will be very lucky if you can find somewhere that suits ***all*** your requirements, and it might be necessary to change your mind on one or two points. You may decide that the advantages of a particular property far outweigh its disadvantages. Remember that the place you choose will be your home. It may not be as "grand" as you would wish, but thoughtful planning and interesting colour schemes and furnishings will brighten the dullest of rooms.

Think and Do

1. Are these sentences ***true*** or ***false***?

a. A person who lives in rented accommodation is called a tenant.

b. A council house is one in which a councillor lives.

c. Local authority rates help to pay for road repairs, libraries and other local expenses.

d. Money for a mortgage can only be borrowed from a bank.

e. A ground rent is paid on leasehold property.

f. A tenancy agreement is the deposit put down on a new house by an owner occupier.

g. Interest is charged on mortgage loans.

h. An unfurnished property is dearer to rent than a similar furnished one.

2. Copy the following diagram into your notebook. Write a suitable sentence in each of the boxes.

3. Visit your school and local libraries and find out all you can on the following. Write a few sentences in your notebooks on each one.

a. Building societies.

b. Council estates.

c. Tied property.

d. Local authority rates and how they are used.

4. List the advantages and disadvantages of renting furnished accommodation for a couple with a young family.

5. Where would you go and what would you do, if you wanted to apply for each of the following?

a. A mortgage.
b. A rent rebate.
c. A council house.

6. Choose one word from column B to complete the sentences in column A.

Column A	**Column B**
a. Money paid to a landlord is called	***mortgage***
b. When money is borrowed for the purpose of buying a property, a ...... is required.	***insured***
c. All property should be ...... against possible damage.	***council***
d. A ...... house is one that is owned by a local authority.	***rent***

7. What expenses would an owner occupier of a new semi-detached house expect to have?

8. Calculate the "rate" bill for each of the following families:

	rateable value	*rate in £*	*rates?*
a. ***Family X***	£268	50p	
b. ***Family Y***	£112	96p	
c. ***Family Z***	£90	73p	

Budgeting an income

The money coming into a household is called ***income*** and the money going out in the form of expenses, is called ***expenditure***. The purpose of budgeting is to balance these two items, so that at no time does the expenditure exceed (grow bigger than) the income.

The national income is budgeted by the Chancellor of the Exchequer and on Budget Day he announces the taxes he will need and the measures he will have to enforce to pay for the country's expenses.

Money earned from a job of work can be paid at the end of each week in the form of a ***wage***, or at the end of each month in the form of a ***salary***. A wage is usually paid in cash (notes and coins) and is given to a worker in an envelope called a wage or pay packet.

A salary is paid in the form of a cheque, which can be cashed at a bank or put into a bank account. Some firms will pay their employees' cheques directly into a bank for them or arrange credit transfers between their banks.

Can you think of any advantages and disadvantages for each of these methods of payment?

The amount of money earned is called the ***gross income*** and from this figure several deductions are made.

1 Income tax. Each working person pays income tax to the government. This is to help to pay for the nation's expenses, such as the cost of the Armed Forces and Civil Defence Services, the building of new schools, hospitals and roads, etc. The amount of money each person pays is calculated by H.M. Inspector of Taxes and is deducted from each individual wage/salary before pay day. This method of collecting taxes is called P.A.Y.E. (Pay As You Earn).

2 National insurance contributions. It is compulsory for each working person to contribute towards the cost of the welfare services and a retirement pension. Formerly this was done by means of stamps on a card for national insurance and a separate deduction for graduated

BIZZ FACTORIES LTD 1 APRIL 1976
ROYAL BANK LIMITED
PAY EARNIE MONEY OR ORDER
THE SUM OF SIXTY POUNDS 00 £60-00

pension but both are now combined. Part of the contribution is paid by the employer, part by the employee. For example, when it was introduced in 1975 the standard rate payable was 5·5% of gross income for the employee and 8·5% for the employer. There is a reduced rate for certain married women and widows, and pensioners do not pay at all. The money goes towards the National Health Service which entitles everyone to free medical attention when necessary and to low-cost dental treatment, eye-testing, etc. It also goes towards benefits for sickness, maternity, widows, unemployment and to a pension on retirement.

3 Superannuation or pension. In addition to government pension schemes many firms have private pension schemes and public bodies in particular run what they call superannuation schemes. A deduction is made from the salary for this and the employer usually makes a contribution too. On retirement the employee receives a pension for life and sometimes a lump sum as well.

When these deductions have been taken away from the gross wage/salary, the amount of money left is called the ***net income.*** It is the net income which should be used when working out a budget.

In many households, there is more than one wage packet or salary to consider. The wife may have a part-time or full-time job and this helps to swell the family income. It is a mistake to rely on the wife's earnings and to include them in the regular family budget. When both husband and wife are working, it is wise to budget on the husband's wage alone, and to use the wife's earnings for extra items that may be needed for the home, or for savings. When this is done there is no hardship if the wife suddenly has to give up work for any reason, e.g. to look after a young family. Similarly, it would be unwise to include the pay from a husband's overtime work or spare time job in the weekly budget. These sources of income are not always reliable and can stop suddenly without any warning, causing great hardship to some families.

If you try to write a list of all the normal family bills that must be paid out of an income, you will be surprised at the length of the list. You will find that most of the bills can be roughly divided into three groups:

A those connected with the ***shell*** of the home;
B those connected with the ***members*** of the family;
C those connected with the ***extras***.

However, remember that this is a very broad classification and can vary from household to household. For example, hire purchase repayments if for essential furniture might be in group A instead of group C.

It is not easy to say what proportion of an income should be spent on each of the groups, because this will vary from family to family. It will depend on:

a the size of the home;
b the size of the family;
c the family's individual needs.

For example, a family living in a two-bedroomed council flat will spend less money on expenses in group A (looking after the shell) than a family living in an owner-occupied four-bedroomed detached house. Can you remember why? Similarly, a family with three young children will spend more money on group B (looking after the members of a family), than a married couple with no children.

Here are some points which might help you when working out a budget.

1 Always consider group A first. Most of these expenses can be calculated in advance. Try to work out a sum of money that will cover heating and lighting expenses, and a sum of money that can be put aside for any maintenance and repair work. Write these down.

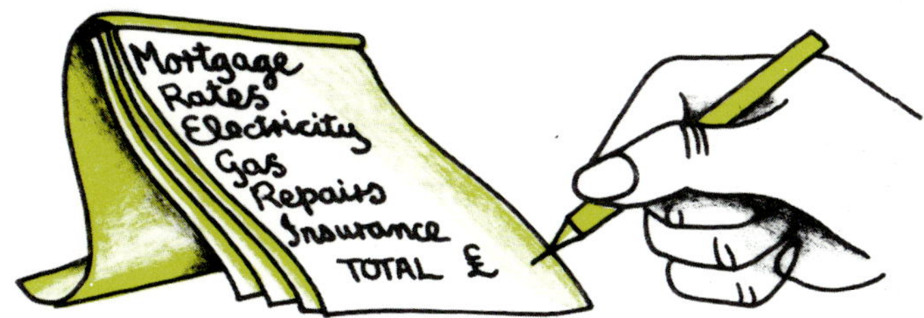

2 When considering group B, remember that a housekeeping allowance will cover more than just food bills. There will be all kinds of cleaning materials to buy, as well

Group A

Expenses connected with the ***shell*** of the home, e.g.
Mortgage repayments or rent,
Rates,
Fuel bills,
Maintenance and repair work of property and furniture,
Insurance of building and contents.

Group B

Expenses connected with the ***members*** of a family, e.g.
Housekeeping,
Clothing,
Travel expenses to and from work,
Children's pocket money,
Children's dinner money (if at school),
Savings (towards holidays, birthdays, Christmas, life-policies, superannuation schemes, old age).

Group C

Expenses that are ***extra***, for luxury items that help to make life easier and more pleasant, e.g.
Car expenses (petrol, road tax, servicing and garage bills),
Telephone bills,
Television rental and licence,
Hire purchase repayments,
Mail order repayments,
Entertainment expenses (smoking, drinking, hairdresser, theatre, football pools, etc.).

as stationery, postage stamps, newspapers, etc. Can you think of any other items? It always helps to see things written down on paper, so make a list of each item in group B and try to work out the requirements for an imaginary family. Start by allowing one third of the weekly net income for food alone, and then add on for these extra housekeeping items. This will give you a rough idea of how much money will be needed for group B, but do remember that this will vary from family to family. In this group you must also allow for clothing expenses, travelling expenses, pocket money and, if possible, a sum of money that can be saved.

3 Group C consists of the non-essential items. If a family finds that it is over-spending and running into debt, it should be from this group that it makes its economies. In some cases, however, a car may be considered an essential part of travel to work and should be included in group B. Any hire purchase agreements should always be allowed for in the weekly expenditure.

4 Remember that some bills will arrive annually (television licence, road tax for car, some insurance premiums, holidays), and unless you have saved towards them, they will come as a nasty shock. Other bills will arrive at different intervals throughout the year. The best way to deal with these irregular bills is to make a complete list of them at the beginning of the year, and to add up approximately how much they will all cost. A regular amount of money can then be put away each week to cover these items.

5 It is not a good idea for a housewife to include the family allowance in her weekly housekeeping money. This is a regular source of income which could be invested in a savings account, or be left to accumulate and used for large expenses, such as children's clothing.

6 Mail order firms offer a comprehensive range of goods which can be bought with credit facilities, or returned if not suitable. Prices are often higher than in the shops, because of the expenses involved in advertising, postage and packing, etc. This type of trading is worth considering for families who do not live near good shopping centres, or who prefer to buy goods in instalments. Mail order repayments should be included in the weekly budget.

7 A housewife should always keep her housekeeping money separate from any personal money.
8 It is often possible to obtain some household goods in bulk, e.g. detergents, groceries. Bulk buying can be economical but do check that large quantities can be stored easily. Remember, too, that you must have enough money to make the large initial outlay, even if the goods bought last a long time.

A word about family income supplements

There are various types of family income supplements and benefits that are available to low income families. If you feel that you or your family may be eligible, consult your social security office, or ask at any post office for details.

Savings

When children are given pocket money they should be encouraged to budget for their weekly needs. If their weekly allowance is spent on the first day, then there is nothing left for the rest of the week. Parents who help out with "loans" and extra pocket money are not helping their children to prepare for adult life. These children may grow up not knowing the value of money, and they may have great difficulty in budgeting an income, when the time comes. Always try to encourage children to save for that "special" toy, or to save towards their holiday spending money. The practice in handling money wisely will benefit them when they grow older.

It is not a good idea to keep money in a money box or home safe for any long period of time. Fire or theft could threaten its safety. There are other forms of saving which are safer, some of which earn interest for the investor.

Think and Do

1. What or who is ***Ernie***? Find out all you can about it/him and write a few sentences on the subject in your notebook.

2. Design a poster that will show people the different ways of saving and investing money.
3. What are the advantages and disadvantages of buying furniture on hire purchase instalments?
4. Imagine that you are single and sharing a furnished, rented flat with a friend. What expenses would you have?
5. Find out where you would go, or what you would do, to:
a. renew a television licence;
b. take out a life insurance policy;
c. apply for welfare milk and vitamins for your baby;
d. query your income tax payments;
e. pay the road tax on a car;
f. complain about interference on your television set;
g. become an organizer for a mail order firm;
h. claim unemployment benefit.
6. What form of saving would you recommend for:
a. a student at a college of technology;
b. a newly-married couple;
c. a schoolgirl;
d. an old-age pensioner?
7. What help and advice can these give to the consumer?
a. The Citizens' Advice Bureau.
b. *Which?* magazine.
c. The Weights and Measures department.
8. Copy the following sentences into your notebook, using the correct word chosen from the words in the brackets.
a. Income tax is deducted from the (***gross, net***) income.
b. A (***current***, ***deposit***) account in a bank does not earn interest.
c. Family allowance is payable for the (***first, second***) child in a family, and all subsequent children.
d. National Savings Certificates can be bought at any (***post office***, ***health clinic***).
e. The national budget is prepared by the (***Prime Minister***, ***Chancellor of the Exchequer***).
f. Buying goods by mail order is usually (***cheaper***, ***dearer***) than buying from shops.
9. What are the advantages and disadvantages of buying goods in bulk?
10. Make a list of the items in a housewife's weekly budget.

Part Two

All about Equipment and Furnishings

CHAPTER 4

Heating a home

The heating of a home is expensive and it is advisable to consider carefully which type of heating system you like best before deciding which one you are going to have.

Heat can warm a room by ***radiation*** or by ***convection***. Radiated heat is heat given off in waves or rays, like the sun's rays, and it warms the objects it touches. Convected heat is heat that circulates and warms the air.

Heating by solid fuel

1 Open fires

An open fire is a welcoming and cheerful sight, especially on a cold, winter's day. It seems to make a room "feel" warm, and the radiated heat is pleasant to the skin. The chimney provides ventilation and this prevents a dry, stuffy atmosphere forming.

An open fire will burn coal, smokeless fuels and wood (oak, ash and beech logs burn well). The ashes and soot formed, create dust and dirt especially when the grate is being cleaned, and this is a disadvantage. There is also a loss of heat which escapes up the chimney, making this type of heating wasteful. Soot and gases are given off and these pollute (spoil) the atmosphere. A strong fireguard should always be placed round an open fire to give complete protection from the flames, especially where young children and old people are concerned or if no one is going to be in the room.

ADVANTAGES

1. GIVES A CHEERFUL ATMOSPHERE
2. WILL BURN MORE THAN ONE TYPE OF FUEL
3. HELPS TO VENTILATE A ROOM

DISADVANTAGES

1. CREATES DUST AND DIRT WHICH POLLUTE THE ATMOSPHERE
2. THERE IS A LOSS OF HEAT UP THE CHIMNEY
3. CAN BE DANGEROUS IF NOT PROPERLY GUARDED

2 Closed stoves

A closed stove burns solid fuel and is a good way of heating a large room. Warm air is circulated around the room by convection currents. The stove doors may also be opened to give radiant heat when needed.

This type of stove is not as cheerful to look at as a blazing open fire, but it is more efficient. There is no loss of heat up the chimney, and the convected heat given off warms the back of the room, as well as the area in front of the fire. A fireguard should be used as the whole stove will get hot.

Smokeless areas

Some councils insist on smokeless fuels being used in all solid fuel appliances to reduce pollution in the air. These areas are called "smoke control areas" or "smokeless zones".

Heating by gas

Gas fires

A gas fire can heat a room by radiation and by convection.

A gas fire looks clean and gives instant heat. A modern gas fire will light automatically at the turn of a switch and can easily be regulated to the degree of heat needed, or turned off immediately it is not required. A radiant gas fire may also have convector channels included, and this type of heater is very efficient and economical, though more expensive to buy. A convector type of gas fire heats a room slowly but evenly. There should always be some ventilation when using a gas fire and for this reason a gas fire will often be fixed into an old chimney breast, or be installed on an external wall with a flue door. Without adequate ventilation, a room heated by a gas fire, is likely to become dry and stuffy and there could be the danger of harmful fumes.

Heating by electricity

1 Electric fires

An electric fire is efficient and easy to use. It can be switched on and off when needed, though the degree of heat cannot be regulated as easily as with gas. It is clean when in use and because it does not need any special ventilation, an electric fire can be moved from room to room. It can also be mounted on a wall if required, or be fixed in a fireplace surround. Some have special "coal burning" effects. The heat from the element of an electric fire is radiant heat but many modern fires also give convected heat.

2 Storage heaters

A storage heater uses off-peak electricity and so is more economical than an electric fire. Electricity is taken in during the night, when it is cheaper to buy, and the heat formed is stored in the storage cabinet and then given off during the day. A separate electric meter has to be installed for use during the off-peak period. A storage heater gives off convected heat and is suitable for cold, draughty areas such as halls and landings, but it does take up quite a lot of room and cannot be easily moved.

3 Infra-red heaters

There is always the danger of electrocution when electrical appliances are used where there is water. For this reason a portable electric fire should ***never*** be taken into a bathroom. An infra-red heater is suitable for this purpose. It should be placed high on a wall and a pull switch attached for safety.

4 Fan convector heaters

A modern fan convector heater is an efficient way of warming a cold room quickly, but it would not be suitable as a continuous source of heat. Some models can be noisy when used and there is a steady "movement" of air, which can be irritating. In summer, a fan convector heater can be used without the heating element switched on, and this provides a flow of cool air to ventilate a hot room. A fan heater uses on-peak electricity.

Heating by oil

A small portable oil stove is useful for heating cold areas of a house. Always buy a reliable, well-known model as a cheap oil stove can be dangerous. Never move an oil stove when it is lighted or place it where it can be knocked over. A good oil stove is reasonably cheap to run and needs little attention, apart from an occasional clean, but obtaining paraffin and filling it can be a bit messy.

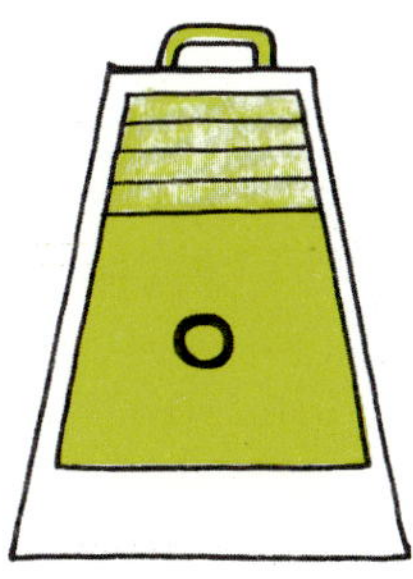

Central heating

Central heating can be ***full*** or ***background***, depending on how hot the temperature becomes in each room. Full central heating means that no other form of heating is necessary. Background heating means that extra heat is needed from some other source.

Many modern houses have some form of central heating included when the house is being built. Central heating usually means that whole or part of a house is heated by radiators filled with hot water coming from a central boiler. This boiler can be fired by solid fuel, oil or gas. A solid fuel boiler has to be stoked and cleaned regularly and can create some dirt, especially when the ashes are being removed. The oil for an oil-fired boiler has to be stored in a tank which must be near to the house and near to the road for easy access by the supply vehicle. A gas-fired boiler is easy to use and there is no fuel storage problem.

Underfloor heating works on a similar principle to the storage heater. Off-peak electricity is used during the night to warm blocks of concrete on the ground floor, and this heat is then given off during the day to warm the house. This type of central heating can only be used in new houses and must be included when they are being built.

Ducted warm air is another form of central heating which can be included when a house is being built. Convected warm air is circulated through special ducts in a room. The movement of air can create dust, though some systems use a filter to prevent this. This type of system can be used in summer with the heating element switched off. In this way it can ventilate and freshen a stuffy, airless room.

Humidifiers

Some types of heaters and heating systems produce a dry, airless atmosphere which is unhealthy, and can cause the furniture, fittings and fabric of a building to deteriorate. Water vapour can be added to the atmosphere by means of a humidifier. There are many different types available, ranging from the electrical fan-blown humidifier to the simple water-filled canister that fits on to a radiator. A bowl of water placed near the source of heat is also effective.

Heating water

Most types of central heating will give hot water from the boiler. Where there is not a central heating boiler, then water can be heated by:

a a solid fuel fire with a back boiler;
b a solid fuel cooking range;
c an electric immersion heater;
d an electric or gas storage heater;
e a gas "geyser". This is usually fixed over a sink or bath, and ***must*** have a ventilation flue. This type gives instant hot water when the tap is turned on.

Often an immersion heater will be provided in a house so that there is an alternative way of heating water in summer, when a central heating system or solid fuel appliance would not normally be in use. Where hot water is stored in a tank, the tank should be lagged, in order to retain as much heat as possible.

Maintenance of heating systems

All types of heaters and heating systems should be serviced regularly to ensure that they are working safely, efficiently and as cheaply as possible. Chimneys to open fires and solid fuel boilers should be swept clean about twice a year. This is an additional expense.

Budgeting for fuel bills

No form of house heating is cheap but some methods are less expensive than others. Try to consider which type of heating is best suited to your home. Visit your local fuel advisory service and find out estimates of running costs for different types of heating systems before you finally decide which kind to have.

When budgeting for fuel bills it is best to consider how much you are likely to spend over a year and then to divide the sum by fifty-two. This will give you an amount of money to save each week towards the cost of heating your home. During the first year, you can calculate roughly what your expenditure is likely to be by asking friends who have similar heating systems. When the bills start arriving, it will be easy to add up what your annual expenditure is going to be. Remember to include all fuel bills. These could be any combination of the following:

a solid fuel bills;
b electricity bills;
c gas bills;
d oil bills.

Fuel bills are paid monthly, bi-monthly or quarterly, but it is still advisable to budget on a weekly basis.

It is always worthwhile to look at doors and windows to see if they are fitting well. Ill-fitting window-frames and draughts from doors can account for a loss of heat which makes any heating system inefficient and wasteful. Where fuel bills are excessive it would be advisable to consider other extra forms of heat conservation, such as roof insulation, double glazing to windows and insulation for cavity walls. These seem expensive at first glance, but they cut down considerably on the heat loss from a home. Always remember to see that pipes and hot water tanks are lagged.

Think and Do

1. List the advantages and disadvantages of an open fire.
2. Use your school and local libraries to find out all you can on the following:
a. off-peak electricity;
b. North Sea gas;
c. pollution of the air by smoke from chimneys;
d. cavity wall insulation.
3. Do a class project on "Keeping warm through the ages".

4. Visit your local fuel showrooms and have a look at the heating appliances available. In your notebook, draw a picture of the one you like best and write a few sentences giving your reasons.

5. Design a poster to encourage people to conserve heat in their homes.

6. Look through magazines and find some pictures of modern gas and electric fires. Stick them into your notebook and underneath each one write the approximate price of the fire and say in which room you would recommend its use.

7. Using a thermometer, take the temperature in your classroom each day for a week, at 9 a.m. and at 1 p.m. Plot your results on a graph.

8. Choose one word from the words in the brackets to complete each of the following sentences. Write the completed sentences into your notebook.

a. A storage heater uses (***on-peak***, ***off-peak***) electricity.

b. In smoke control areas, (***coal***, ***smokeless fuels***, ***peat***) should be burned on open fires.

c. Infra-red heaters are suitable for heating (***lounges***, ***halls***, ***bathrooms***).

d. An (***immersion***, ***emersion***) heater will heat water.

e. Hot water tanks should always be lagged to prevent the loss of (***air***, ***heat***, ***water***).

f. A fan heater works on the principle of (***radiated***, ***convected***) heat.

9. Copy out this crossword and complete it.

Clues across

1. This will heat a room from a central boiler.
2. A fuel.
3. This type of room heater uses off-peak electricity.

Clues down

4. A hot water cistern should always be ....
5. This is formed when coal burns.
6. Can fuel a central heating system.
7. This should be used wherever there is an open fire.
8. This heater will heat water.

Sink units

If you stop to consider the different types of jobs that are associated with the kitchen sink, you will realize how important it is to have a well-designed and efficient model. A busy housewife will use the sink not only for washing up but for preparing food such as fruits and vegetables. She will use it when washing clothes and when collecting water for household cleaning jobs. The sink may also have to cope with childrens' dirty hands that frequently need washing especially after playing in the garden, hose pipes that need to be connected to the taps when washing the car or watering the plants, and kettles that need to be filled when making a cup of tea.

It is obvious then that a sink unit should not only look attractive, it should also be efficient to use and to keep clean.

If you are in a position to choose a new sink for your kitchen, then visit a showroom and look at a selection of models. Consider the height of each unit. A sink should be slightly higher than the other working surfaces in a kitchen because most of the work is done halfway down the bowl.

It would be most uncomfortable to be always bending over a sink that is too low.

Look for a sink that will be easy to clean. It should not have any awkward corners, gaps or ledges that can collect dirt and germs. A well-designed sink unit has the draining board and sink bowl moulded in one piece, and has a "splash-back" to prevent water from dripping down the walls behind the unit.

A sink may have one or two draining boards depending upon the size of the kitchen and the lay-out of the working surfaces. Some sinks have two bowls. These are really only suitable for large kitchens, and are expensive to buy.

A sink should be hard-wearing. It will be used continually and it should be able to stand the occasional knock and bang from heavy saucepans. Always choose a deep sink in preference to a shallow one. It is more convenient to use and there is less danger of flooding the kitchen floor when washing clothes or emptying bowls of water.

A modern sink unit can be made from several different types of material. Probably the most popular material is ***stainless steel***. This is a hard-wearing substance that looks attractive and is easily cleaned. A stainless steel sink can be moulded in one piece with a single or double draining board and this eliminates a dirt trap. Because metal is a good conductor of heat, a stainless steel sink is quickly warmed by hot water and this prevents grease sticking to the sink during washing up.

A sink can be made with a ***vitreous enamel*** finish. This type of sink can be bought in a variety of colours and designs. It looks attractive, is easy to clean but can chip with constant hard wear. A vitreous enamelled sink is moulded in one piece with the draining board and usually has a splash-back.

A sink can be made with a white ***porcelain*** finish. This type of sink is hard-wearing but stains quickly. A porcelain sink does not have draining boards moulded on. A free standing draining board of wood, steel or enamel is often attached but there is always a danger of dirt and germs collecting under the joint, unless constant attention is given to cleanliness.

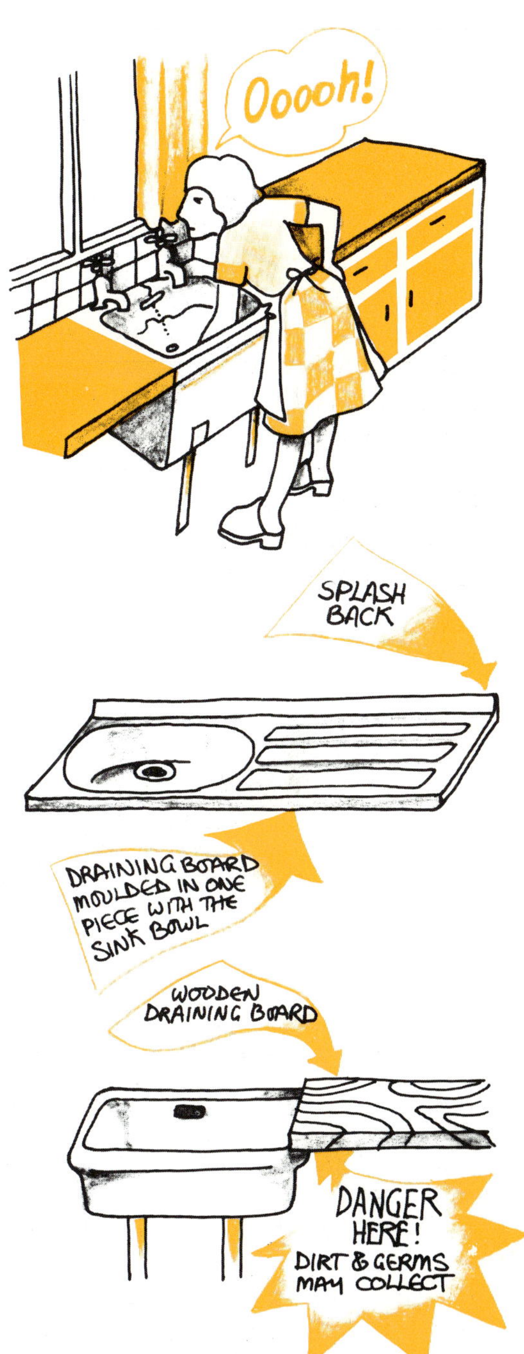

A sink can also be made of ***plastic*** but this roughens through time and becomes difficult to keep clean.

Most taps are chromium-plated and have an easy clean cover. Some modern taps are made from coloured polymer and remain cool even when running hot water. Shapes can vary and some taps are easier to turn on and off than others, especially when hands may be wet or greasy. Some sinks have "mixer" taps. With these taps, hot and cold water can be mixed to the right temperature and run from one central tap. Can you think of any advantages and disadvantages of this type of tap?

Taps should not be too near the bottom of the sink because this makes the filling of jugs, buckets and bowls difficult.

Most sinks have an overflow outlet just below the rim of the sink. This is to prevent floods occurring if the taps are left open and the plug-hole becomes blocked. Water should drain down the overflow outlet rather than on to the kitchen floor. Do watch for dirt collecting in the outlet hole. It should be kept ***clear*** and ***clean*** always.

A modern sink unit will have cupboards built underneath and usually a deep drawer for storing cutlery. These can be very useful. Look for a recess at floor level, so that it is possible to tuck one's toes underneath, when standing at the sink unit. It can be very uncomfortable and bad for the posture if you have to tilt forward to reach the bottom of the sink.

If you move into a house or flat and find that the kitchen sink is not as modern-looking as you would have wished, do not despair. Many faults can be remedied. A sink top that is open underneath can be easily "boxed-in". A do-it-yourself enthusiast will quickly fit hinged or sliding doors across the space, so giving the impression of a built-in unit. A simpler remedy is to drape plastic or cotton material around the sink on a curtain wire. This can look very attractive and is easily removed for cleaning.

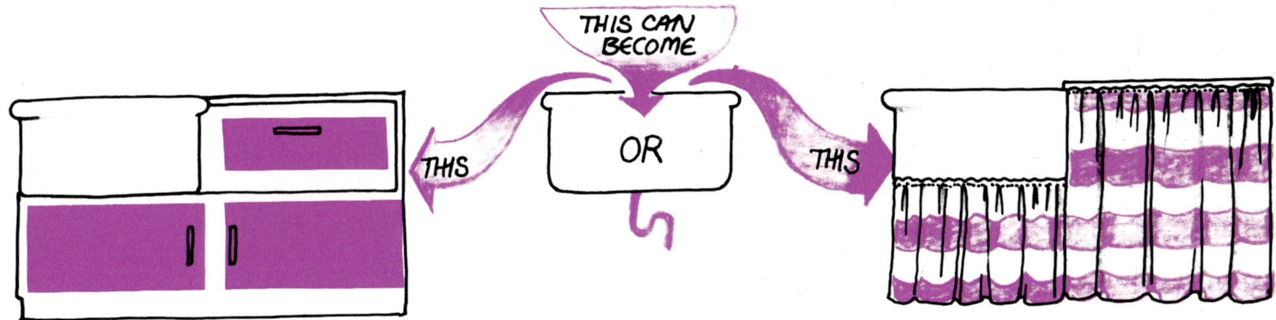

An old wooden draining board can be disguised by covering it with a colourful, plastic-coated paper. The wall behind and above the sink may need some protective covering if there is not a good splashback. Vinyl paint and vinyl-coated wallpaper wipe down easily and are very suitable for use in a kitchen. Tiles of many different finishes, colours and designs can be bought to fix on wall surfaces that are frequently splashed. These are readily cleaned and can add colour and gaiety to a kitchen.

Most kitchen sinks are placed under a window. There are many reasons for this. An attractive or interesting view from a window can make tedious jobs more pleasant. A window will throw light on to the sink and this makes chores like peeling vegetables easier on the eyes. A window provides ventilation. This will be appreciated when standing at the sink on a hot day, or when steam from the washing machine or cooker collects in the kitchen.

Underneath the sink is a pipe that takes the waste water from the sink into the drains. About 10cm below the sink, the pipe bends into a "U" shape. This is called a ***trap***. The water which collects in the trap acts as a barrier and prevents gases, unpleasant smells and insects coming into the house from the drains and sewers. If the trap should get blocked with bits of food, tea leaves, etc., it may be cleared by unscrewing the nut at the bottom of the U bend, and letting the contents of the trap empty into a bucket. It is important to keep clean, fresh water in the U bend. This prevents the smell of stale water from escaping through the plug-hole into the kitchen. After using the sink, let clear water run from the tap for a few minutes. This will rinse out the sink and fill the trap with fresh water.

Some of the more modern sinks have a plastic screw-cup instead of the U bend and this is easier to clean out.

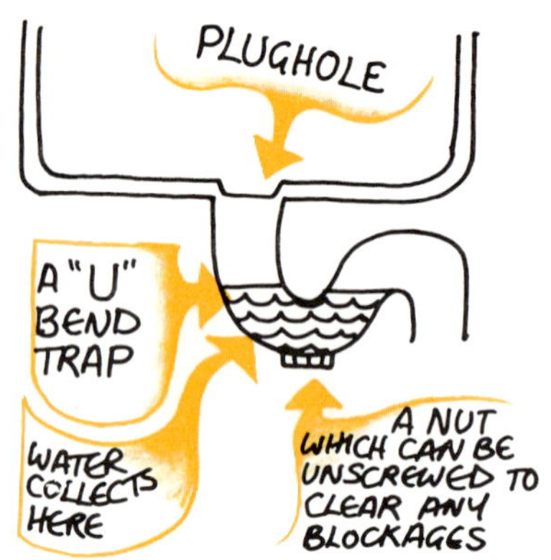

How to keep a sink clean and fresh

It is a good idea to invest in one or two "extras" to help to keep your sink clean, uncluttered and efficient to use. These accessories are not expensive to buy and can be obtained in a variety of colourful and hard-wearing materials. ▶

Here are some points to remember.

1 A sink should always be kept clean. It is a good idea to form the habit of rinsing the sink bowl with hot water whenever it has been used. Wipe behind the taps and around the overflow outlet. Wipe down the draining board, paying attention to any corners or dirt traps.

2 Grease should be removed immediately by washing down with detergent and hot water.

3 Do not allow bits of food and other rubbish to collect in the plug-hole or to block the pipe. Use a sink basket or kitchen waste bin for all these scraps.

4 Stains can be removed from most sinks by rubbing with a little detergent sprinkled on a wet cloth. A cleansing paste, a little bleach or a small amount of scouring powder on a wet cloth, can be used to wipe off very stubborn stains. Remember, though, that scouring powder is an abrasive and will scratch any surface so this must be used sparingly. Avoid using it on stainless steel sinks. A cleansing paste or detergent is milder and will not dull or scratch the shiny surface of the metal.

5 Wooden draining boards need to be frequently scrubbed. Care should be taken to clean into corners and grooves.
6 Very dirty water (e.g. after mopping the floor) should be poured down the outside drain or down the lavatory and not into the kitchen sink.
7 Do not chip or scratch a sink by using heavy metal buckets and bowls. Plastic ones are cheaper to buy, more attractive to look at and lighter to use.
8 It is a good idea to rinse a little disinfectant down the drain daily. This will help to keep the pipes fresh and clean.
9 Washing soda should be rinsed down the sink once a week. This helps to remove any grease that might be lining the pipes.
10 Keep the outside drain cover clear of garden rubbish and litter. If this is allowed to collect, it will prevent water from the sink running down into the drains. It will also encourage germs and insects.

Washing up

Always be methodical and work tidily, when washing up. Here are some points to help you.
1 Remove any scraps of food from the plates and scrape them into a sink basket or waste bin. Stack the plates and dishes near the sink.
2 Empty tea leaves and coffee grains into a sink basket. Liquid fatty waste should be poured into a dish and left to solidify. It can then be scraped into some newspaper and put in the dustbin.
3 Collect all cutlery and place it in a pile near the sink.
4 Run hot water into the sink or into a bowl. Add a small amount of washing-up liquid or detergent.
5 Using a dishcloth or a brush, start to wash up. Wash the cleanest things first such as glasses and cups. Stack each item tidily in the plate rack. Take care not to chip or crack glassware on the taps.
6 Care should be taken with cutlery. Check that the prongs of forks are cleaned thoroughly. Cutlery handles that are made of wood or bone should not be immersed in hot water. Hold them in your hand while washing only the metal parts.

7 Casserole dishes and saucepans should be washed last. Any stubborn stains can be removed with a cleansing paste or with scouring powder.
8 Collect a jug of hot water (not too hot) and pour it over the crockery and cutlery in the plate rack. This will rinse off any remaining detergent. Leave everything to drain in the plate rack or dry it on a clean towel.
9 Empty the sink basket into newspaper. Wrap up the rubbish and place in the dustbin. Wash the empty sink basket clean.
10 Empty the dirty, soapy water down the sink. Wipe the plate rack, draining board and taps dry. Rinse out the dish-cloth and hang it up to dry. Rinse the sink with hot water. Hang up the tea towel to dry off.

Think and Do

1. What points would you look for when buying a new sink?
2. Find out all you can about the water supply in your area. In your notebook, write a paragraph on:
a. how and where it is collected;
b. how it is treated and purified;
c. how it is piped to your home.
3. Find out the current prices of each of the following:
a. a block of household soap;
b. a linen tea towel;
c. a polythene sink basket;
d. a canister of washing-up liquid;
e. a nylon pan scourer;
f. a strong disinfectant;
g. a small packet of washing soda;
h. a large plastic bucket.
4. Look in magazines and find a picture of a modern kitchen. Stick it into your notebook. Underneath the picture write whether or not you like the choice of sink. Give reasons for your opinion.

5. Imagine that you have just entertained some friends to the following meal: grilled sausages, chipped potatoes, baked beans; fresh fruit salad; lemonade. Say in what order you would ***a.*** clear the table and ***b.*** wash up the crockery, cutlery and saucepans you have used.

6. How would you dispose of:

a. tea leaves;

b. liquid waste fat from a frying pan;

c. dirty water after mopping the floor;

d. garden rubbish that has collected on the outside drain cover?

7. Copy this diagram into your notebook and write an appropriate sentence in each of the boxes.

8. Say what is meant by the following terms:

a. scouring powder;

b. U bend trap;

c. washing-up detergent;

d. overflow outlet;

e. mixer tap;

f. splashback.

Cookers

Choosing a new cooker is not easy and a visit to your local fuel advisory showrooms will probably bewilder you. There are so many different types and styles of cookers available today and so many new features to choose from, that you may wonder just where to begin.

It is important to know how much money you can afford to spend on a cooker. This will limit the number of models you can consider, and so make the selection process simpler. You must also restrict your choice to the size of cooker that will fit into your kitchen but check that it is big enough to cope with your family's requirements, before making a final decision.

A modern cooker can be fuelled by ***gas***, ***electricity*** or ***solid fuel***. Your choice may depend upon the area in which you live and the availability of the fuel. Gas and electric cookers are easy to use and to keep clean, and the fuel is readily available in most areas. Solid fuel cookers have the advantage of being able to heat the domestic water supply in addition to the cooking, but they are not so clean as gas and electric cookers. Can you think of any other advantages and disadvantages for each type of cooker?

When you have decided on:

a the amount of money you can spend;

b the size of cooker that you need;

c whether you prefer a gas, electric or solid fuel cooker;

then your task of choosing a particular model will be much easier.

Gas cookers

A gas cooker consists of a hob, an oven and a grill.

a The hob. This is the name given to the gas rings or burners on a gas cooker. A modern gas cooker usually has four burners. Gas burners light automatically from a central pilot light, when the gas taps are turned on. The burners and pilot light are set into a sealed vitreous enamelled tray. This makes the hob easier to clean. Some gas rings can be thermostatically controlled so that the correct heat for simmering, boiling and frying can be used. This can save the busy housewife time and energy. She need no longer watch for the saucepan of milk that boils over, or clean up after it has happened.

b The oven. The oven to a modern gas cooker is usually heated by a back burner. This can be ignited automatically from a pilot light, or by the push-button method. Some models use a gas poker for lighting the oven. The heat inside an oven is controlled by a thermostat. The thermostat is turned to the gas mark required and this regulates the heat inside the oven. A gas cooker can have a fully automatic oven that will switch itself on and off at pre-set times. This is an invaluable aid to the busy housewife and to the housewife who goes out to work. Many modern gas ovens are fitted with a safety feature called the flame failure device. This instrument stops the flow of gas into the oven, if the burner goes out. Some types of gas cooker have double ovens, and a new concept is the dual gas and electric cooker which has a gas hob combined with an electric fan-heated oven. A gas oven may have vitreous enamelled sides

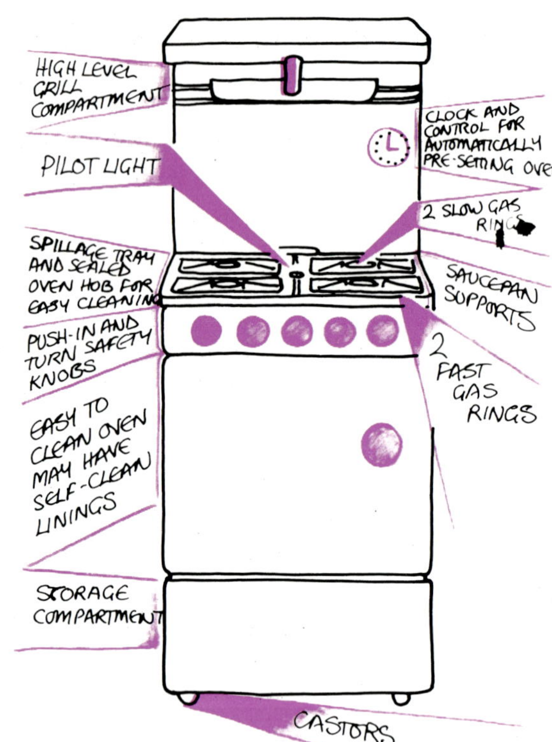

which are easy to clean, or it may have a self-cleaning lining. The oven shelves can be moved into different positions when needed, and the door of the oven sometimes has an inner glass lining.

c The grill. Some models have the grill compartment at waist level, just below the hob of the cooker, and some models have a high level grill. Do check that you can comfortably reach the grill before deciding to buy a cooker. High level grills are not convenient for short people and tall people find waist level grills uncomfortable to use. A grill will light automatically from a pilot light or with the push-button method, or it may have to be lighted with a gas poker or lighter.

If you are interested in buying a gas cooker, visit your local gas showroom. Look at the various models in your price range and select the one that you think suits your requirements best. The picture shows a modern gas cooker with a high level grill.

Care and cleaning of gas cookers

Use your cooker sensibly. Do not try to cook food too quickly, e.g. water that is boiling vigorously in a saucepan will splash on to the cooker, but water that is boiling gently will not.

Here are some points to help you when cleaning a gas cooker.

1 Wipe up spills and splashes at once using a damp cloth or sponge-backed pad. Splashes which have burned on to the surface of the cooker may need special attention. Always try hot water and detergent first. If these fail, then try a cleansing paste or scouring powder, but take care not to scratch the surface of the enamel.

2 Wipe over the inside of the oven after it has been used and while it is still warm.

3 The hob of a gas cooker is sectional and can be dismantled for cleaning purposes. ***Remember to switch off the pilot light before you do this. The hob will be hot.***

4 Wash the burners, saucepan supports and grill pan in the sink, using hot water and a detergent. Rinse well and dry each part thoroughly.

5 Wash and dry the spillage tray on the cooker hob.
6 Replace the burners and saucepan supports. Light the pilot light and test that each burner will light automatically. If a burner has become blocked, use a spent matchstick to clear the hole.
7 Wipe around the knobs and over the remaining surfaces with a damp cloth. Dry well.

Electric cookers

An electric cooker consists of a hob, an oven and a grill.
a The hob. This is the name given to the hotplates on an electric cooker. A modern electric cooker usually has four radiant hotplates. Some models have one or two hi-speed hotplates which will heat up very quickly. Other models have a themostatically controlled hotplate which will remain at the temperature selected until it is switched off. This ensures that foods are not over-cooked and that liquids, such as frying oils, do not overheat. A new feature introduced into some electric cookers is the "dual ring" hotplate. This consists of two rings one inside the other, which can be switched on separately or together, depending upon the size of saucepan being used. The smaller ring is used for small saucepans and the larger ring is only switched on when a large saucepan is being used. This economy feature is well worth considering. Some hotplates are hinged and lift up to allow easy cleaning of the drip tray and vitreous enamel hob. Other electric cookers have a removable spillage tray that can be easily wiped over, when necessary. With an electric cooker it is advisable to use saucepans that have a solid, thick base. These are more efficient and durable.
b The oven. The oven of a modern electric cooker is heated by elements which are usually fixed in the sides of the oven. The degree of heat is controlled by a thermostat, which can be set to the required temperature. Some modern electric cookers have the element at the back of the oven and a fan which helps to circulate the heat. The fan speeds up the heating process and cooking time, and gives an even heat throughout the oven. The sides, roof and base of the oven are usually removable and are easily cleaned, or you

can buy a model that has self-cleaning liners fitted. Some electric cookers will automatically clean themselves by burning off any dirt. Oven shelves can be moved into different positions when needed and the door of the oven sometimes has an inner glass lining. An electric cooker can have a fully automatic oven that will switch itself on and off at pre-set times. Some electric cookers have double ovens. The smaller oven, sometimes called an ovenette, is more economical to use when cooking individual dishes and the larger oven can be used when cooking several dishes.

c The grill. The grill may be at waist level or at a high level. Some waist level grill compartments have extra elements fitted and can be used as a second smaller oven. This is more economical than heating the larger oven when only cooking one dish. All modern electric cookers have large grill pans which can usually be placed in several positions, giving different speeds of cooking.

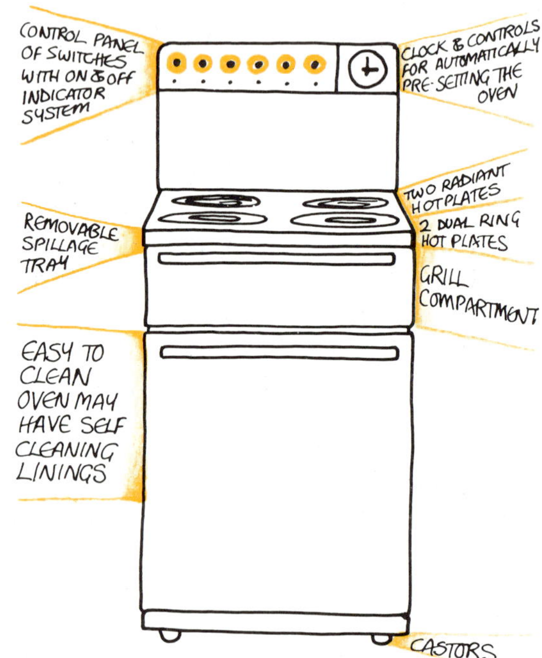

If you are interested in buying an electric cooker, then visit your local electricity showroom. Look at the various models in your price range. Remember that electric cookers work at the turn of a switch, so choose a model that has a clear indicator system to show which hotplates have been switched on and off. The picture shows a modern electric cooker with a waist level grill compartment.

Care and cleaning of electric cookers

Always turn the cooker off at the main switch before starting to clean.

1 Wipe up spills and splashes at once, using a damp cloth or sponge-backed pad. Obstinate stains which have burned on can be removed with a paste or scouring powder.

2 Wipe over the inside of the oven after it has been used, while still warm, unless it has a self-clean lining.

3 Remove the spillage tray and grill pan and wash in the sink, using hot water and a detergent. Rinse well and dry.

4 The hotplates can be scrubbed with a scouring pad or steel wool if necessary.

5 Wipe around the knobs and over the remaining enamel surfaces with a damp cloth. Dry well.

Split level cookers

It is possible to buy a gas or electric cooker in two separate units. The hob can be fitted on to a cupboard top or work surface, and the oven can be installed at a convenient height elsewhere in the kitchen. The main advantage of this type of cooker is that the high level oven is more convenient to use and easier to clean. It must be remembered that split level cookers are more expensive to buy and install, than free-standing ones. Here is a kitchen with one.

A new idea in split level cooking is the ceramic hob. This consists of a large flat sheet of white ceramic glass, under which lies the heating elements. The position of the heating elements is indicated by a circular pattern on the ceramic sheet. This type of hob is tough, heat resistant and very easy to clean.

Spit cooking

A rôtisserie attachment is included or can be bought with some electric and gas cookers. This attachment has a rotating spit which is ideal for spit roasting poultry and joints of meat. Some rôtisseries have rotating skewers for cooking kebabs, sausages, kidneys, etc.

Solid fuel cookers

A modern solid fuel cooker will burn coal, coke, or any kind of smokeless fuel. Remember, however, that smokeless fuels are cleaner to use than coal and help to reduce pollution in the atmosphere. A solid fuel stove will heat the domestic water supply, in addition to the cooking, and will also give heat to the kitchen. A modern solid fuel cooker is well designed and is easy to use and to keep clean. It consists of a hob, an oven and a fire-box.

a The hob. The hob or hotplate of a solid fuel cooker has an insulating, hinged lid which can be lowered to retain the heat. There is usually a fast and a slow cooking area to the hotplate, so that boiling and simmering temperatures can be obtained when cooking.

b The oven. Some models have two ovens, one of which is a cool oven and useful for the slow cooking of stews and casseroles. A modern solid fuel cooker has an oven thermometer but the temperature cannot be regulated as efficiently as with a gas or electric oven.

c The fire-box. The fire-box can be open or enclosed. The rate of burning in the fire-box can be controlled by various dampers and draught excluders, and there is an ash pan below the grate to be emptied periodically. Here is a modern solid fuel cooker.

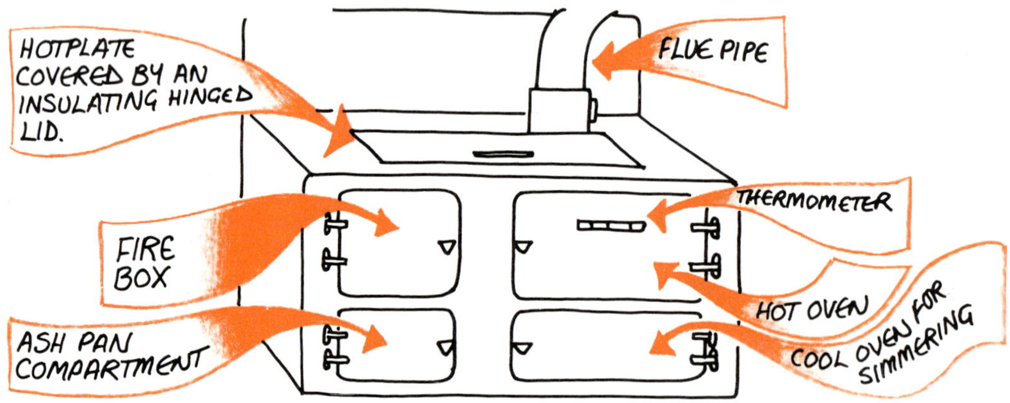

Care and cleaning of solid fuel cookers

1 Rake the fire-box and re-fuel. Empty the ash pan. Brush the oven free of dirt.

2 Wipe up spills and splashes using a damp cloth or sponge-backed pad. A cleansing paste or scouring powder will remove stubborn stains from the hotplate.

3 Wipe the enamelled surfaces with a damp cloth. Dry.
4 Rub over handles and any metal parts with a dry duster.
5 Flues should be cleaned regularly. Follow the instructions for each model, when emptying the flue boxes.

Servicing schemes

A cooker is an expensive piece of equipment, so do look after it. Many manufacturers of cookers run their own servicing schemes and customers may join if they wish to, on payment of an annual fee. The scheme usually offers regular servicing of a cooker, and repair work when necessary. Alternatively, your local electricity board will service an electric cooker and your local gas service centre can arrange for the servicing of a gas cooker. The repairing and servicing of a solid fuel cooker should be referred to the manufacturer.

Think and Do

1. Collect pictures of cookers from magazines. Stick them into your notebook under the heading "Cookers of today".
2. How would you:
a. remove a milk stain from a cooker top;
b. arrange to have a gas cooker serviced;
c. give a weekly clean to a solid fuel stove?
3. What type of cooker would you recommend for a cold kitchen in a farmhouse? Give reasons for your choice.
4. Have a good look at a modern electric cooker that has an automatic timer for the oven. Read the instructions carefully and then see if you can set the dials for the following:
a. After 3 hours delay . . . . heat up to 180°C (350°F) for 1½ hours.
b. After 5 hours delay . . . . heat up to 200°C (400°F) for ¾ hour.
c. After 6 hours delay . . . . heat up to 220°C (425°F) for 1 hour.
d. After 4 hours delay . . . . heat up to 170°C (325°F) for 2½ hours.

5. Find out all you can about the following and write a short paragraph about each:

a. flame failure devices;
b. oven thermostats;
c. self-cleaning oven linings;
d. split level cookers.

6. Visit your school and local libraries and find out all you can on "Cookers through the ages". Prepare a classroom display.

7. Are these sentences ***true*** or ***false***?

a. An automatic oven will switch itself on and off at pre-set times.
b. A high-speed hotplate can only be used when simmering.
c. The flues of a solid fuel cooker should be cleaned regularly.
d. Always wipe over the inside of an oven when it is cold.
e. A cleansing paste should be used to clean vitreous enamelled surfaces.
f. A solid fuel cooker will burn coal or any kind of smokeless fuel.
g. A modern gas cooker can be lighted automatically by a pilot light.
h. A fan-heated electric oven takes longer to heat up to any set temperature.

8. Copy out this crossword and complete it.

Clues across

1. This can help to heat an electric oven.
2. A numbered dial on a cooker.
3. The hotplates are here.

Clues down

4. A solid fuel stove will heat this.
5. A type of cooker.
6. Is formed when solid fuel is burned.

9. Imagine that you have just bought a new electric cooker. What equipment will you need for its daily care and cleaning?

10. Plan a complete dinner that you could cook using just the hob of a gas cooker.

Washing machines and the family wash

A wash day used to be a hard, dreary day for housewives but today's range of labour-saving laundry equipment has made it much easier.

Let us consider the different ways of doing the family wash. A housewife can:

Automatic washing machines

An automatic washing machine is expensive to buy but many people consider it to be a worthwhile investment. Its main advantage is that the washing can be loaded into the machine and then left, and the complete washing, rinsing and spinning programme will proceed automatically. This is obviously an excellent idea for the working housewife, who can go out to her job knowing that the family wash will be done in her absence. Many people who do not go out to work appreciate the freedom that using an automatic washing machine can give them: they can go shopping or do other household tasks while the machine is coping with the washing. Can you think of any other advantages?

An automatic washing machine is more efficient if it is plumbed into the domestic water supply. This leaves the taps free and also saves time in connecting and disconnecting the filler hoses.

There are many types of automatic washing machine available and it is wise to collect as much information as possible about each model before deciding to buy any particular one. Some automatics have a better reliability and servicing record than others, and it is important that such an expensive piece of equipment should work efficiently, so do ask around for advice. Why not read the appropriate article in the Consumers' Association magazine *Which?*

There are some semi-automatic washing machines which go through the various stages without the clothes having to be touched. The controls do not work automatically and someone must be present from time to time to operate the switches and knobs. A semi-automatic washing machine is cheaper to buy than a fully automatic one.

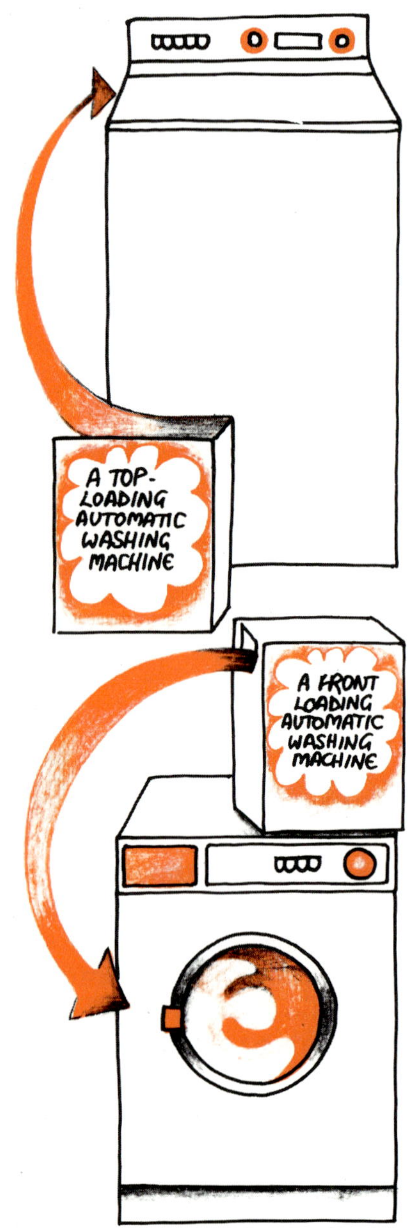

Points to look for when choosing an automatic washing machine

1 It should be easy to load. Some automatics have a top loading door and others have a front loading "port-hole". Front loading machines can fit snugly under a working surface but do check that there is ample room to open and close the door. A few front loading machines have a soap dispenser on the top, which means that they can only be used under a detachable working surface.

2 It should be quiet when in use. Some automatics can be very noisy when working. A complete washing programme can vary in length from $1\frac{3}{4}$ hours to 4 hours, and a prolonged continuous noise would be very annoying.

3 It should conform to safety standards. There are new regulations governing the opening of doors while washing is in progress. Check that the model you choose has the B.E.A.B. safety mark (see page 154).

Twin tub washing machines

A twin tub washing machine is cheaper to buy than most of the automatics, and it will cut washing time to a minimum.

Two loads of washing can be treated at once: one load in the wash tub; the other in the spin dryer.

A twin tub washing machine can be pushed under a working surface, or can be stored in any convenient place and then wheeled close to the sink when needed.

Clothes from the wash tub have to be transferred to the spinning compartment by hand and a pair of laundry tongs is essential for this task. Clothes can be rinsed while they are in the spinner. The washing action can be by a side pulsator/activator or a central agitator.

Again remember that some models have a better reliability and servicing record than others, so do ask around for advice before buying.

Points to look for when choosing a twin tub washing machine

1 It should have a good-sized wash tub. A twin tub washing machine does not have as big a wash tub as an automatic, but it should take about 2 kilos (dry weight) clothing.

2 It should have a heater. Most twin tub machines will heat cold water but this can be extravagant with electricity. To economize, fill the wash tub with hot water and then use the heater to boil or get the required temperature.

3 It should be easy to empty. Check that it is not difficult to empty water from the wash tub and from the spin tub. Some hoses are more convenient to use than others.

4 It should be easy to keep clean. There should not be awkward lips and ledges that will trap water and dirt. Check that the washing machine can be wiped dry easily.

5 It should conform to safety standards. There are regulations governing the lifting of the lid while the spinner is in motion. Check that the model you choose has the B.E.A.B. safety mark (see page 154).

Single tub washing machines

A single tub washing machine can be bought in different sizes. There is a small-sized machine which will take the same load as a twin tub washer, medium-sized machine, and a large one whose load capacity is equivalent to that of an automatic. It is possible, therefore, to choose the size of washing machine that will suit your particular needs. All the models cost less than an automatic washing machine and the small single tub washers are cheaper than twin tubs. Ask as many opinions as possible before purchasing, as reliability and servicing vary a lot.

A single tub washing machine can be pushed under a working surface or it can be bought with a special lid that will give extra working space in the kitchen. It is light, easy to move and simple to operate. Most models have a heater, and all single tub washers can be emptied automatically. The washing action can be by a side pulsator/activator or a central agitator.

Care and cleaning of washing machines

Always switch off and remove the plug before starting to clean a washing machine. A washing machine should be wiped over and dried thoroughly after being emptied. All removable parts should be lifted out and wiped dry. Filter trays should be cleaned.

A washing machine is an expensive piece of equipment, so do look after it. Manufacturers of washing machines run their own servicing schemes and customers may join if they wish to, on payment of an annual fee. The scheme usually offers regular servicing and any repair necessary.

Wringers

A wringer is made to fit a particular single tub washing machine. It is light-weight, easy to assemble and simple to operate. It can be either hand driven or power driven.

Do check that a wringer has a safety mechanism that will release caught clothes or trapped fingers.

After use, a wringer can be stored inside the wash tub or in a separate compartment underneath.

Separate spin dryers

A spin dryer can be a useful addition to laundry equipment. It can be used to dry clothes that have been washed by hand, or clothes that have been washed in a single tub washing machine. A spin dryer gets clothes damp dry.

There are two types of spin dryer: pump operated models and gravity operated models. A pump model is more expensive than a gravity one, and is easier to operate. The water is pumped straight into the sink through a hose. A gravity model is emptied through a spout or outlet at the front of the dryer, and the water has to be collected in a bucket or bowl. Do check that the spout on a gravity model is high enough to allow room for a bucket underneath.

Using a laundry

Some people like to use a laundry for the larger items in the family wash, such as bed-linen, table-linen, shirts, etc. This can save washing, ironing and airing time but is rather expensive. Can you think of any other advantages and disadvantages of sending clothes to a laundry?

If you wish to send clothes to a laundry:

- ***a*** check that all pockets are empty;
- ***b*** remove any coloured clothes that might "run";
- ***c*** mend any tears;
- ***d*** tie all the clothes together securely.

Always keep a list of the clothes you are sending and then it is easy to check that they have all been returned later. Any obstinate stains should be mentioned and then these can be given special attention at the laundry.

Using a launderette

A launderette can be used for several different reasons. It can be used in emergencies when a washing machine or dryer has broken down, or it can be used when wet clothes cannot be dried outside because of bad weather. A launderette usually has large tumble dryers which can be used for getting clothes really dry, much drier than with a spin dryer. Many people use the launderette for bulky items that they do not want to wash by hand or cannot fit into their own washing machine at home, e.g. thick blankets, quilts and eiderdowns. Some people use the launderette regularly because they do not have a washing machine at home. For them the weekly visit to the launderette can be a social occasion when they meet friends and chat while waiting.

Clothes can be taken to a launderette for:

a washing;
b washing and drying;
c drying only;
d dry cleaning.

If you wish to use a launderette, check that you are not including in the wash any coloured clothes that might run. Remember to:

a check that all pockets are empty;
b mend any tears;
c ask if any of the buttons and buckles should be removed from garments that are to be dry cleaned.

Washing by hand

If you do not have a washing machine, it would be wise to try to wash a few things by hand each day. This will make the task much easier. If you spend a few minutes every morning or evening washing the odd item, it will prevent the washing from accumulating. You may wish to consider sending the larger, more difficult items to the laundry, or taking them to the launderette.

Laundry accessories

The modern housewife has many aids that she may use when tackling the family wash. Wash care labels, which are attached to most clothes and furnishing fabrics, give advice on the washing procedure needed in each case. With these, and today's variety of washing powders, detergents, bleaches, fabric conditioners and starches, there is no excuse for unsuccessful laundrywork.

1 Wash care labels

The Home Laundering Consultative Council (H.L.C.C.) has worked out a series of labels giving simple washing instructions for the different fabrics (see page 56).

For an automatic washing machine, set the dial(s) to correspond with the label number, and the correct washing procedure will be followed. If you are using a twin tub or single tub machine, follow the directions given under the "machine" heading, and if you are washing by hand, follow the instructions given under the "hand wash" heading.

The continental system of textile labelling uses the following signs and symbols:

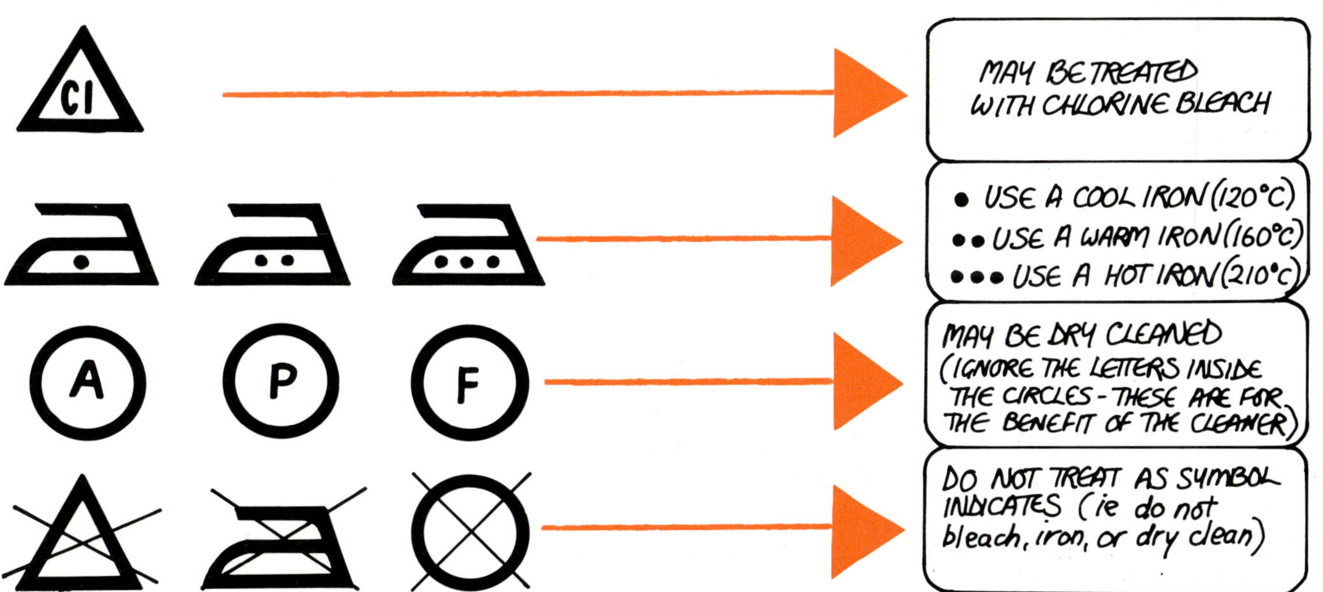

MACHINE	HAND WASH
Very hot to boil maximum wash	Hand-hot or boil
Spin or wring	

White cotton and linen articles without special finishes

MACHINE	HAND WASH
Hot maximum wash	Hand-hot
Spin or wring	

Cotton, linen or rayon articles without special finishes where colours are fast at 60°C

MACHINE	HAND WASH
Hot medium wash	Hand-hot
Cold rinse. Short spin or drip-dry	

White nylon; white polyester/cotton mixtures

MACHINE	HAND WASH
Hand-hot medium wash	Hand-hot
Cold rinse. Short spin or drip dry	

Coloured nylon; polyester; cotton and rayon articles with special finishes; acrylic/cotton mixtures; coloured polyester/cotton mixtures

MACHINE	HAND WASH
Warm medium wash	Warm
Spin or wring	

Cotton, linen or rayon articles where colours are fast at 40°C, but not at 60°C

MACHINE	HAND WASH
Warm minimum wash	Warm
Cold rinse. Short spin. Do not wring	

Acrylics; acetate and triacetate, including mixtures with wool; polyester/wool blends

MACHINE	HAND WASH
Warm minimum wash	Warm Do not rub
Spin. Do not hand wring	

Wool, including blankets and wool mixtures with cotton or rayon; silk

MACHINE	HAND WASH
Cool minimum wash	Cool
Cold rinse. Short spin. Do not wring	

Silk and printed acetate fabrics with colours not fast at 40°C

MACHINE	HAND WASH
Very hot to boil maximum wash	Hand-hot or boil
Drip-dry	

Cotton articles with special finishes capable of being boiled but requiring drip drying

HAND WASH
See garment label

Articles which must not be machine washed

Do not wash.

2 Washing powders and detergents

SOAP POWDERS
These are made from animal and vegetable fats. They get clothes clean, do not remove colour, and 'lather' well. They are easy to rinse out. Their main disadvantage is that they form scum when used with hard water. Suitable for hand washing and single and twin tub machines.

SYNTHETIC DETERGENTS
These are made from synthetic ingredients mainly hydrocarbons. They get clothes clean and lather well. They do not form scum when used with hard water. Clothes washed in synthetic detergents sometimes feel harsh. Suitable for hand washing and single & twin tub machines

LOW LATHER DETERGENTS
These are designed for automatic washing machines especially front loaders

"SOFT" DETERGENTS
Pure soap flakes and liquid soap are suitable for delicate fabrics. They are easy to rinse and leave clothes feeling soft. Suitable for hand washing

NON IONIC DETERGENTS
These are very good for removing grease and oil from heavily soiled clothes. Suitable for handwashing, single and twin tubs, automatics

ENZYME DETERGENTS
These break down protein stains and so are good for cleaning food stained articles. Very effective in a hand hot soak or pre-wash. Do not use when boiling. This will destroy the enzymes. Suitable for hand washing and single & twin tub machines

ALWAYS RINSE YOUR HANDS IN COLD WATER AFTER USING ALL WASHING PRODUCTS

3 Bleach

Bleach is used to keep white cottons and linens looking bright and clean. It should not be used on coloured fabrics. Can you think why not? Always be careful when handling bleach. It should never be used in a concentrated form but should be diluted with cold water. To brighten white cottons and linens, soak them overnight in a solution of bleach in cold water. Stains can be removed by soaking the fabrics in a stronger solution of bleach and cold water. (The strength of solution may vary with different bleaches, so do read the directions given on the bottle.)

4 Fabric conditioner

There are several fabric conditioners which can be added to the final rinsing water, when washing clothes. These conditioners "relax" fibres. They make clothes feel springy and soft, and help to prolong their life.

5 Starch

Starch is used to keep cottons and linens looking crisp and fresh. Clothes that have been starched keep clean longer by resisting dirt. Starch can be bought:

a in a powdered form (ordinary or instant);
b in a liquid form;
c as a spray.

Always read the directions given. Ordinary powdered starch can be made in different strengths to suit particular garments. The crispness from liquid plastic starch remains for several washes, so this type of starch need not be used each wash day. Spray starch is convenient and economical to use because the spray can be directed at the particular parts of a garment that need to be starched, e.g. collars and cuffs. Try to make a list of the household linens and personal garments that are improved when starched.

6 Water softener

A special substance can be used to soften hard water. A water softener prevents scum from forming when using soap, and this means that less washing powder is needed for the family wash. Sodium carbonate (washing soda) can be used to soften water, or a special water softener and conditioner can be bought.

Planning the family wash

How you set about doing the family wash will depend upon the type of laundry equipment you have to help you.

If you have an automatic washing machine, there is no need to set aside any particular day as a wash day. Wait until you have a full load of the same type of fabric, i.e. coloured cotton and linen, then programme the machine for the correct wash group (see H.L.C.C. code) and leave. When the washer has switched itself off, you can re-programme the machine for another group of fabrics. If you have not got a full load for another group, then leave the rest of the washing until you have. It is extravagant to run an automatic washer with just a quarter or even half a load. The odd garment that may be needed in a hurry, should be washed by hand.

If you have a twin tub or single tub washing machine, you will need to set aside an hour or more for doing the family wash. You will have to be around to work the controls and transfer the clothes to the spin dryer or sink (for rinsing), but there is no need to stand and watch the washing machine do the work for you. Arrange to do other jobs while you are waiting for each stage in the washing programme. You may wish to wash the pots, prepare vegetables for the next meal, make the beds or just have a cup of coffee while you read the newspaper. Remember that the kitchen floor will probably get splashed when you are handling the wet clothes, so it would be a good idea to mop it after you have finished and put the washing machine away.

If you are doing the family wash by hand, you will be advised to wash small amounts frequently. This will make the task easier. Try to leave the clothes to soak for a few hours (overnight would be best). This will make the clothes easier to wash and will save a lot of harsh rubbing. If you cannot arrange to have sheets, blankets, curtains, etc. washed at the laundry or launderette, kneel down and wash them in the bath. You will find that they are easier to handle in the larger space.

If you go out to work, you may wish to:

- ***a*** do the family wash during an evening;
- ***b*** get up early one morning and do the wash before you go to work;
- ***c*** wash at the weekend;
- ***d*** save up and buy an automatic washing machine;
- ***e*** use a laundry or launderette.

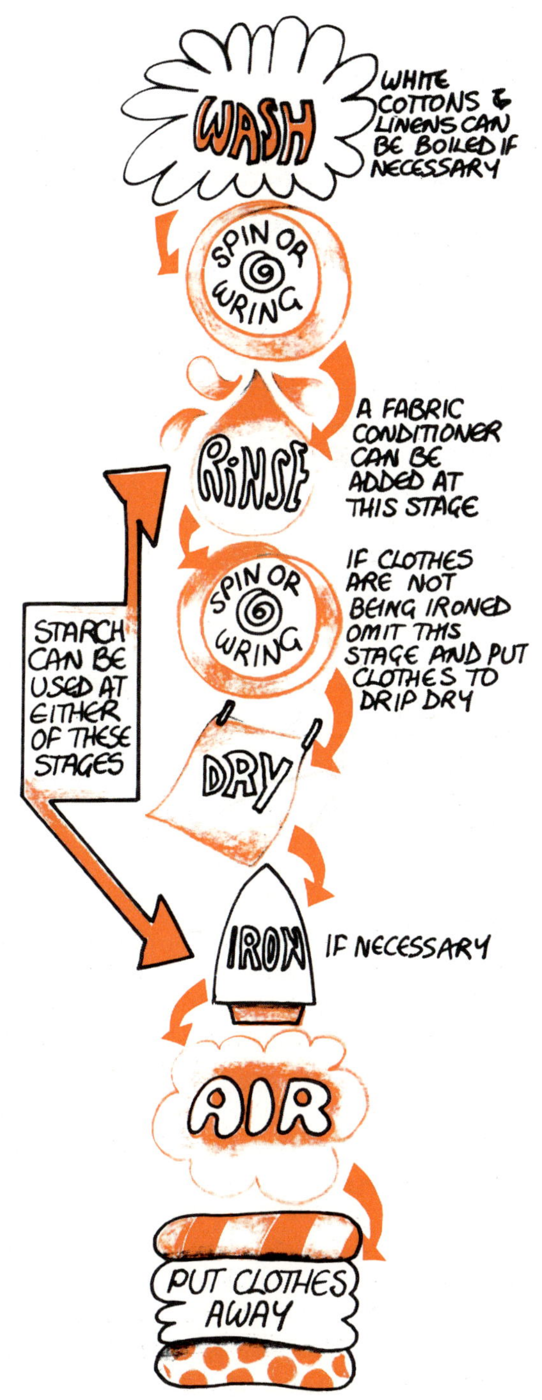

Doing the family wash

There are certain preparations that should be done before you start to wash.

1 Check garments. Do check that all pockets are empty. Any tears should be mended before you wash, and any loose buttons sewn on.

2 Remove any bad stains. This can be done by:

- ***a*** rinsing in cold water;
- ***b*** soaking in warm soapy water;

c soaking in a cold bleach solution (only suitable for white cottons and linens);
d soaking in warm water with an enzyme powder (in an automatic washer this is the pre-wash stage);
e using a special solvent or stain remover (always read the instructions carefully).

Here is a chart showing some common stains and the special solvents needed for their removal.

Stain	Treatment	*Points to remember*
Blood, egg and non-greasy food stains	Soak in cold water or use an enzyme washing powder. After treatment, rinse well or wash in the normal way.	
Grass	Use methylated spirits. After treatment, rinse well or wash in the normal way.	*Methylated spirits should not be used near a naked flame. It is INFLAMMABLE.*
Greasy food stains, oil and lipstick	Use carbon tetrachloride or a special grease solvent. After treatment, rinse well or wash in the normal way.	*Carbon tetrachloride should only be used in a well-ventilated room or in the open air. It has a poisonous vapour.*
Paint a oil-based	Use turpentine or a turpentine substitute. After treatment, rinse well or wash in the normal way.	*Paint stains must be removed immediately.*
b emulsion	Rinse in cold water or use methylated spirits.	
Nail varnish	Use acetone or a special nail varnish remover. After treatment, rinse well or wash in the normal way.	*Acetone is INFLAMMABLE. Do not use near a naked flame. Always test a small piece of fabric with the solvent to check that there will be no damage.*

3 Sort into groups. If you are doing the full family wash, sort out the clothes into piles according to the H.L.C.C. wash labels (see page 56) and to their colours. Remove any articles whose colours may run. These must be washed separately. Using the correct temperature of water, and the right powder/detergent, start to wash each group of clothes.

Stain	Treatment	*Points to remember*
Ink and iron mould	Soak in a solution of citric acid or lemon juice. After treatment, rinse well or wash in the normal way.	
Coffee and tea	Soak in warm, soapy water or use an enzyme washing powder. For dried stains, rub with glycerine before soaking in a solution of sodium bicarbonate or borax. After treatment, rinse well or wash in the normal way.	
Mildew and obstinate fruit stains	Soak in a solution of hypochlorite bleach. After treatment, rinse well or wash in the normal way.	*Only white fabrics can be treated in this way. Do not use on wool or silk.*
Chewing gum, bubble gum and tar	Scrape off as much as possible. Soften the stain by rubbing with grease, e.g. lard, butter. Use carbon tetrachloride or a special grease solvent. After treatment, rinse well or wash in the normal way.	

Drying clothes

Clothes can be dried in many different ways.

Irons

Nearly all irons are electric now and have a heat control on them. Some irons are lighter to handle than others but these may give a less satisfactory finish to the garment. Heavy irons, provided they are not too heavy to handle, usually give a better result. An iron with a smaller base plate and a sharply-pointed tip is good for ironing fine garments and for getting into corners and gathers. A steam iron is very useful as it can be used either dry or filled with water. The water comes out as steam and helps when pressing garments. When a dry iron is used for this, a damp cloth can be put over the garment or it can be sprinkled with a little water first. Choose the type of iron that you think will suit you best.

Before ironing always switch on the iron and let it heat up. Turn the heat control to the correct setting. Some irons are marked with the H.L.C.C. grades and some use the International Textile Care Labelling Scheme. In this system heat control is graded as 1 dot, 2 dots and 3 dots.

Always keep the iron upright when not in use and remember to switch off and take the plug out after use. A steam iron should be filled when cold and emptied after use. Do read the manufacturer's instructions carefully. Always keep the sole plate of the iron clean. A rub with steel wool will remove marks which might stain garments.

Ironing boards

It is possible to iron anywhere, e.g. on the floor or on a table, provided you do so on a thick padding such as a piece of folded blanket with a sheet, but it is best to purchase an ironing board. These can be easily assembled, adjusted for height, and usually have a well-padded cover which is removable for washing. They are shaped so that garments can be drawn over them, ironed, turned round and another bit ironed, without causing any creasing. A sleeve board can be bought separately or is sometimes part of an ironing board. This is the same shape as the ironing board but much smaller, and is useful when pressing sleeves.

Ironing

Many items in the family wash will not need to be ironed.

Towels
Some types of bed linen
Some types of table linen
Nappies
Most items of underwear
Socks and stockings
Drip-dry clothes

Do not need ironing

Items that need to be ironed should be:

- ***a*** ironed when damp;
- ***b*** dried completely and then damped down;
- ***c*** dried completely and ironed with a steam iron.

Garments that require a cool iron (check the H.L.C.C. label) should be ironed first. Set the thermostat on the iron to the correct position. Increase the temperature of the iron when needed. Iron cottons and linens last of all, because they will need a hot iron. Always iron a garment until it is dry. If you are using a spray starch, spray it on, then iron immediately.

Try to iron with long sweeping movements. Take care not to iron a garment or item out of shape. For example, if you start with a square handkerchief it should finish square and not distorted.

If ironing a garment such as a shirt or blouse it is best to work in the following order:

- ***a*** collar;
- ***b*** sleeves and cuffs;
- ***c*** one side of the front;
- ***d*** back;
- ***e*** the remaining side of the front.

Airing

After ironing garments such as shirts and blouses, it is probably best to leave them loose to air. When folding them to put away:

- ***a*** fasten all buttons;
- ***b*** place the garment front side downwards;
- ***c*** fold each side and sleeve inwards to overlap across the centre back;
- ***d*** fold upwards once or twice from the bottom of the garment.

Clothes should be thoroughly aired before they are put away. Use:

- ***a*** the airing cupboard;
- ***b*** a radiator (clip on rails are a good idea);
- ***c*** a clothes dryer;
- ***d*** a clothes "horse".

Think and Do

1. Copy the chart of H.L.C.C. wash care labels (page 56) into your notebook.
2. List the advantages and disadvantages of using:
a. an automatic washing machine;
b. a twin tub washing machine.
3. Invent a name for a new "miracle" detergent. Either, design a poster advertising your new product, or design its packaging.
4. How would you:
a. remove a coffee stain from a cotton tablecloth;
b. starch the collars and cuffs of a shirt;
c. keep nappies soft and fresh?
5. What advice would you give to a working mother on doing the family wash?
6. Try to visit a laundry or launderette. Write an illustrated account of what you saw.
7. Collect empty packets of as many different soap powders/detergents, as you can. Prepare a classroom display of laundry accessories.
8. Imagine that you have just done a family wash using a single tub washer with a wringer. Say how you would dry your clothes.
9. Visit your school and local libraries and find out all you can on:
a. enzyme washing powders and how they work;
b. laundry equipment of the 19th century;
c. hard and soft water.
10. Look at a selection of irons when you next go shopping. Feel them and price them. In your notebook describe which one you liked best and give reasons for your choice.

Refrigerators and freezers

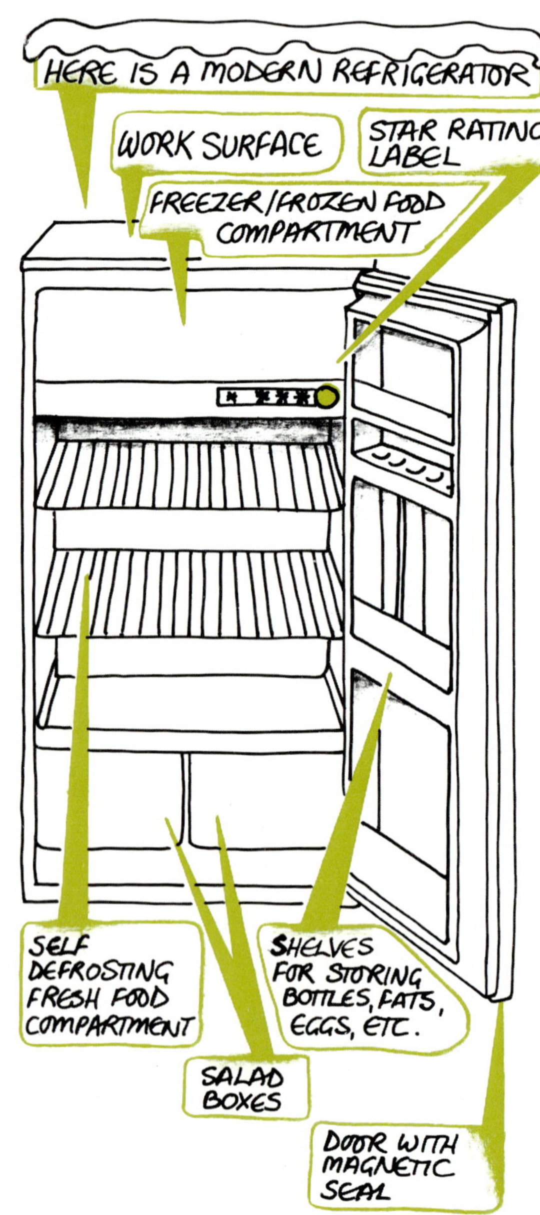

A refrigerator is a well-insulated cabinet that will keep food cold. Food that is kept cold will keep fresh longer than food stored at normal room temperatures. This is because the germs and bacteria which cause food to go bad, can only multiply ***very***, ***very slowly*** in cold surroundings.

Is a refrigerator really necessary?

Food can be kept cool by using:

- ***a*** a well-ventilated larder with a cold slab;
- ***b*** a cellar;
- ***c*** a food safe in the open air, sheltered from sunshine;
- ***d*** a refrigerator.

A refrigerator is therefore not essential, if you have other satisfactory ways of keeping food cool.

The advantages of having a refrigerator

A refrigerator is an expensive piece of kitchen equipment which some people still class as a "luxury". When used properly, though, a refrigerator can be a valuable asset in a busy household.

1 It will keep food fresh and full of flavour.

2 A refrigerator reduces the amount of food that is wasted, because "left-overs" can be stored safely and used another day.

3 Large amounts of food can be bought and stored, and this cuts down on shopping time.

4 A whole range of exciting cold dishes can be prepared.

5 A selection of frozen foods can be stored in a special compartment. These need little preparation and can save time and energy in making hurried meals.

How a refrigerator works

A household refrigerator works on the principle that when a ***liquid*** changes into a ***gas***, there is a cooling effect, and heat is absorbed from the surroundings. This continuous cooling effect draws heat from the food which is in a refrigerator, and so keeps it cool.

The different types of refrigerator

There are many different types, sizes, colours and designs in modern refrigerators. A visit to your local gas and electricity showrooms will prove this.

A refrigerator has a frozen food compartment which can be used to make ice-cream, ice-cubes, etc., and to store ready-frozen foods. The frozen food compartment has a star rating, which is usually printed on the outside of the compartment door. This indicates for how long ready-frozen foods should be stored in that particular refrigerator.

Ready-frozen foods can be stored for up to 1 week

Ready-frozen foods can be stored for up to 1 month

Ready-frozen foods can be stored for up to 3 months

A frozen food compartment is ***not*** suitable for freezing fresh food and for the long term storage of ready-frozen foods. For this you need a freezer.

Points to remember when using a refrigerator

Here are some points to help you when using a refrigerator.

1 Always keep the door closed, so that the inside of the refrigerator is kept as cold as possible.

2 Never put warm food in a refrigerator. (Can you think why not?)

3 Only put ***clean*** food in a refrigerator. Salad vegetables should be washed before being stored.

4 All foods should be covered, especially liquids. Greaseproof paper, aluminium foil and special "cling" films can be used for wrapping and covering foodstuffs. Plastic storage boxes can be used, and are suitable for strongly-smelling foods.

5 Do not over-pack a refrigerator. Always allow room for the cold air to circulate.

6 If there is a power cut, keep the refrigerator door ***closed***. Food will keep fresh for up to 8 hours, in a closed refrigerator. After 8 hours, the refrigerator must be emptied, and the food used as quickly as possible.

7 When going away on holiday and leaving the refrigerator turned off, always leave the door ***open***. This will allow air to circulate and will keep the inside of the cabinet fresh.

8 Do not use a refrigerator for storing bananas, root vegetables, apples or onions. It is not necessary to store eggs in a refrigerator, but if they are, they should be taken out and allowed to reach room temperature before being used.

Here is a diagram to show you the best positions for storing foods in a refrigerator.

Defrosting and cleaning a refrigerator

When a refrigerator is working, ice is formed which builds up around the frozen food compartment. This has to be removed periodically, so that the refrigerator can operate efficiently and economically. Most modern refrigerators defrost automatically, either with the push-button method or with a self-defrost mechanism. (Self-defrosting refrigerators need no special attention because the water formed from the melting ice is evaporated.)

To defrost an ordinary refrigerator:

1 Either switch off or turn the controls to the defrost position.

2 Remove the ice-cube trays and wash out.
3 When the ice has melted from the frozen food compartment, empty the drip tray.
4 Wipe the inside of the refrigerator with a damp cloth and then wipe dry.
5 Re-fill the ice-cube trays with cold water and replace in the frozen food compartment.
6 Switch on the refrigerator or turn the controls to normal.

It is not necessary to empty food from the cabinet or the frozen food compartment if the refrigerator has a high-speed defrosting mechanism. If you are in doubt, refer to the instruction booklet.

If a refrigerator is wiped over periodically, there should be little special cleaning needed. It is a good idea to wash down the inside of the cabinet occasionally with bicarbonate-of-soda in warm water. This will freshen the refrigerator and remove any smells. The outer surface of the refrigerator should be washed with warm, soapy water, and then dried thoroughly. Handles and decorative panels should be rubbed with a soft, dry duster.

Freezers

Refrigerators can be bought that have a freezer/frozen food compartment. These are clearly labelled:

This type of refrigerator ***can*** be used for freezing fresh food and for the long term storage of ready-frozen foods.

Separate freezers or deep freezes, as they are sometimes called, can be bought that will either team up with an ordinary refrigerator, or be free-standing. A freezer can have sliding shelves or deep pull-out baskets for the storage of frozen food (see page 70).

A separate freezer is useful, if:

1 You have home-grown produce which you want to keep fresh.
2 You live a long way from the shops, and need to buy and store large quantities of "perishable" foods.

3 You like to bake in bulk and store dishes for a long time.
4 You entertain regularly and like to keep a good store of "perishable" foods and prepared dishes.
5 You like to buy fruit and vegetables in season (therefore cheap), in large quantities.
A freezer is ***not*** a good investment if you only intend using it for storing bought ready-frozen foods.

Servicing schemes

A refrigerator or freezer is an expensive piece of kitchen equipment, so do take care of it. Many manufacturers run their own servicing schemes and customers may join if they wish to, on payment of an annual fee. The scheme usually offers regular servicing, and repair work when necessary. Alternatively, your local electricity board will service an electric refrigerator, and your local gas service centre can arrange for servicing a gas refrigerator.

Think and Do

1. How can you keep food fresh, if you do not have a refrigerator?
2. Prepare a class display on "Food storage through the ages". You may find some history textbooks helpful.

3. Visit a local supermarket and look at the range of ready-frozen foods. Prepare a list of frozen foods that a housewife might buy when planning for the:
a. Christmas period; ***b.*** summer school holidays.
4. Collect pictures of modern refrigerators. Stick them into your notebook and underneath write a few sentences on the care and cleaning of refrigerators.
5. List the advantages of having a refrigerator with a freezer/frozen food compartment.
6. Say how you would:
a. get rid of a stale smell from a refrigerator;
b. defrost an ordinary refrigerator;
c. store salad ingredients in a refrigerator.
7. Find out the current prices of:
a. a packet of 10 fish fingers;
b. a roll of "cling" film wrapping paper;
c. a small packet of frozen puff pastry;
d. plastic food storage canisters;
e. a combined refrigerator/freezer suitable for a large family;
f. "loose" frozen peas.
8. Visit your school and local libraries and find out:
a. about food poisoning;
b. how a refrigerator works.
9. Copy the following diagram into your notebook under the heading "Star ratings for refrigerators".

Ready-frozen foods can be stored for up to ***1 week***

Ready-frozen foods can be stored for up to ***1 month***

Ready-frozen foods can be stored for up to ***3 months***

10. Look through a selection of recipe books and find a recipe for home-made ice-cream. Prepare the dish and then work out the approximate cost of the ingredients. How does the flavour and texture compare with bought ice-cream?

Floor coverings

Covering the floor areas in your home can be a confusing and costly experience. It is wise to look around the shops, obtain expert advice and think carefully, before deciding on any particular floor covering. There are many types available in many different qualities, and the temptation is to buy the covering that looks attractive to the eye. This may not be a sensible purchase. Each room in a home should be thought about separately because each area has its own problems. Let us consider the qualities of a good floor covering.

Types of floor covering

1 Carpets

It is always wise to buy the best quality that you can afford. It is not economical to buy a cheap carpet that will wear so badly that it has to be changed after a few years. If you must economize when buying a carpet, do so in rooms that do not get much hard wear, such as bedrooms. A good quality carpet is essential in lounges and in well-trodden areas, such as halls. A carpet can create a sense of warmth and comfort. It muffles sounds, helps to insulate a room against draughts and gives a non-slip, easy to clean surface.

A carpet can be "fitted" to the shape of a room, or it can be free standing as a bound or fringed carpet square. A fitted carpet can make a room look bigger by "pushing out" the walls but it has the disadvantage that it cannot be turned to give even wear. With a carpet square, the carpet can be turned regularly and this will prolong its life. Carpet tiles help to solve this problem. The tiles can be lifted up and moved about to avoid excessive wear in any one place, and obstinate stains can be hidden under furniture.

The main fibres used in carpet making are: ***wool***; ***nylon***; ***acrylic***; ***rayon*** and ***hair***. A wool carpet is warm, resilient, very hard-wearing and will not easily soil. It is not affected by static electricity, as many man-made fibres are, but it is expensive to buy. A nylon carpet is tough, hard-wearing and easily cleaned, but it will show the dirt quickly. Dust will cling to the surface due to static electricity. An acrylic carpet is warm and resilient but soils easily, like nylon. It is easy to clean. A rayon carpet does not wear as well as other types of carpet and is a cheaper fibre. It is not recommended for areas of heavy use. A hair carpet is made from animal fibres, such as goats' hair. It is a cheaper type of carpet which is very hard-wearing, but it does show stains easily. Many carpet manufacturers make carpets from a mixture of fibres. A blend of 80% wool and 20% nylon gives a carpet that has all the advantages of wool, coupled with the hard-wearing qualities of nylon. There are other blends of materials available, which are worth considering when choosing a carpet.

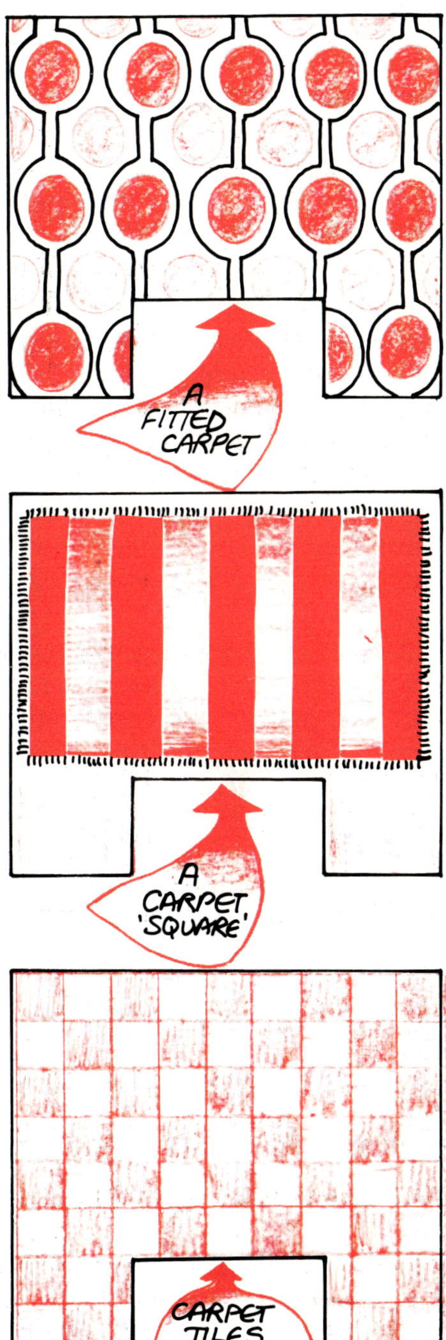

A carpet can be made in different ways. It can be ***woven***, ***tufted***, ***corded*** or ***bonded***. Axminster and Wilton carpets are woven on looms. An Axminster carpet is available in a variety of colourful patterns but a Wilton carpet is plainer and uses fewer colours. A tufted carpet costs less than a woven one and it can be made from a wool/nylon mixture or from nylon and acrylic fibres. The pile, which can be looped or cut, is stitched into a backing. A cord carpet is woven in tight loops which give it its hard-wearing properties. A bonded carpet is made from polypropylene, nylon or other fibres. The fibres are needled into a backing giving a flat, felt-like floor covering which is very hard-wearing. A bonded carpet is water-repellent and this property makes it a good floor covering for bathrooms and kitchens.

A carpet needs an underlay. An underlay prolongs the life of a carpet by protecting it from rough floor surfaces and from dust that creeps up between the floorboards. It will also improve the "feel" of the carpet by adding thickness. An underlay can be made of:

- ***a*** felt;
- ***b*** foam rubber;
- ***c*** a composition of felt bonded to foam backing.

Some carpets are made with a built-in foam rubber underlay. This type of carpet does not require a separate underlay.

If you are buying a carpet, choose the colour carefully. Remember that a floor surface is a large area. A brilliantly gaudy pattern could look effective on a rug but may be very overpowering on a fitted carpet. A self-coloured carpet may blend in well with other furnishings but it will show marks, bits of thread, fluff, etc. easily, and should be avoided in living areas. A self-coloured carpet can be more safely used in bedrooms.

When choosing a carpet, do check that it is suitable for the type of wear it is likely to get. Most carpets are graded to suit particular areas in a home. If you are in doubt, ask the shop assistant for advice. The British Carpet Centre labels most woven carpets as suitable for light, medium or heavy usage. Good quality tufted carpets are labelled by the Teltag Scheme, which gives advice on usage and carpet care, and most leading carpet manufacturers supply their own labelling plan.

2 Vinyl floor coverings

There are many colours and exciting patterns available in today's range of flexible, vinyl floorings. Vinyl floor coverings can be bought as individual tiles or in sheet form.

Vinyl is a very hard-wearing substance which is easy to keep clean. It does not show stains. These properties make it a good floor covering for bathrooms and kitchens. Cushioned vinyl has its own built-in underlay. This makes the vinyl even more hard-wearing and resilient and gives a softer, warmer floor covering. The textured surface of the cushioned vinyl makes it slip-proof, which is an important point to remember when covering slippery areas such as bathroom floors.

3 Linoleum
Linoleum is a hard-wearing and resilient floor covering. A good quality linoleum will outlive a vinyl floor covering but it requires more cleaning and is dearer to buy. The pattern can be "inlaid" or printed on the surface. Inlaid linoleum wears far better than printed linoleum. There is a wide range of colours in plain, marbled, mottled and wood grained effects.

4 Wood
A wooden floor is hard-wearing and gives a warm, rich effect to a room. Wood is expensive to buy but when compared to the price of a fitted carpet, there is little difference. A modern wooden floor needs little attention and should last a lifetime. Many different woods can be used (oak, maple, teak, beech, etc.), and many patterns can be laid.

The main disadvantage of a wooden floor is that it can become slippery if highly polished or if it is splashed with water.

There are many other floor coverings which you may wish to consider. Clay and ceramic tiles, cork and brick are other examples. Have a look at the latest ideas in floor coverings and try to think of the advantages and disadvantages for each one.

Suitable floor coverings for each room
1 Kitchen
The kitchen is probably the most used area in a house. The floor covering in the kitchen must be very hard-wearing.

It is important that it is also easy to clean and that it does not become slippery when wet. It should be resilient enough to withstand abrasives (scouring powders), and chips, cracks and knocks from dropped objects. A good kitchen flooring should look cheerful and feel comfortable. Some modern floor tiles, e.g. ceramic tiles, have the disadvantage of looking and feeling cold and hard.

Here are some suitable floor coverings for a kitchen:

a a good quality bonded carpet;
b a good quality vinyl (tiles or sheet);
c cushioned vinyl.

2 *Living room*

The floor covering chosen for a living room will depend upon the size and age of the family. A family with young children will need a very hard-wearing floor covering that will not show stains easily, but a couple with no children may choose a more elegant covering that is not as durable. Remember that patterned surfaces do not show stains as readily as plain ones, and a living area may have to cope with spilt drinks, cigarette ash, as well as dirt and mud from shoes. The floor covering in a living room should be warm and comfortable.

Here are some suitable floor coverings for a living area:

a a fitted good quality woven carpet;
b a fitted 80% wool 20% nylon carpet;
c a fitted good quality tufted carpet;
d carpet tiles;
e a wooden floor, with a carpet square or scatter rugs.

3 Dining room

In a through lounge/dining room the floor covering should be continuous. This helps to make the room look bigger. A separate dining room can have a different floor covering from that in the lounge. It is important that spilt liquids, food crumbs and stains can be easily dealt with, and that the floor covering is not slippery. Remember that though the flooring should be durable, there will be far less wear and tear in a dining room than in other areas in a home.

Here are some suitable floor coverings for a dining room:

- ***a*** good quality vinyl tiles;
- ***b*** carpet tiles;
- ***c*** ceramic tiles;
- ***d*** a bonded carpet;
- ***e*** a wooden floor.

4 Bedrooms

It is possible to economize when covering bedroom floors. These are areas which do not have much hard wear and many cheaper floor coverings are suitable. Remember, though, that a bedroom floor should feel nice and warm to bare feet.

Here are some suitable floor coverings for bedrooms:

- ***a*** a wool/man-made fibre mixture carpet;
- ***b*** an acrylic carpet;
- ***c*** a rayon carpet;
- ***d*** a tufted carpet;
- ***e*** a bonded carpet;
- ***f*** a polished floorboard surround with a carpet square;
- ***g*** a linoleum surround with a carpet square.

5 Hall and stairs

These are areas that need a very hard-wearing floor covering. It is also important that the flooring will not show dirt readily and that it can be easily cleaned.

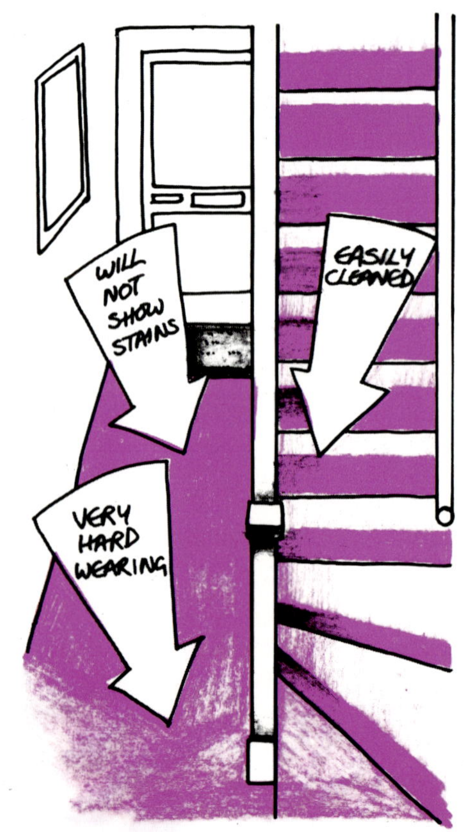

Here are some suitable floor coverings for halls and stairs:

- ***a*** a Wilton, Axminster or tufted carpet;
- ***b*** a hair cord or sisal carpet;
- ***c*** carpet tiles (not for stairs);
- ***d*** a patterned vinyl (not for stairs);
- ***e*** an inlaid linoleum (not for stairs);
- ***f*** a wooden floor with rush mats (not for stairs).

6 Bathroom

It is important that a bathroom floor should not be slippery, and that it should feel warm to bare feet.

Here are some suitable floor coverings for a bathroom:

- ***a*** a cushioned vinyl;
- ***b*** a patterned vinyl (tiles or sheeting);
- ***c*** a bonded carpet;
- ***d*** a man-made fibre carpet.

The care and cleaning of floor surfaces

Carpets. It is normal for a new carpet to shed fluff. For the first three months, use a stiff brush to keep the carpet clean. When a carpet has stopped shedding fluff, it should be cleaned daily with a carpet sweeper or vacuum cleaner. Any marks and stains should be treated immediately.

- ***a*** Rub gently with a damp cloth, working from the outer edge of the stain to the middle. Obstinate stains can be rubbed with warm water and detergent, or a special carpet cleaning fluid.
- ***b*** Rub with a dry cloth.

Rugs and carpet squares should be turned frequently. This will prolong their life by evening out the wear. Carpets and rugs can be shampooed when necessary. Use either a carpet shampooer with a special cleaning fluid, or warm water and detergent. ***Do not overwet a carpet.*** Allow all carpets to dry thoroughly before replacing furniture.

Vinyl floor coverings. These should be swept and washed regularly. Use warm water and detergent, or a special floor cleaning liquid. Only non-slip polishes should be applied.

Linoleum. Linoleum should be dusted regularly. Wash occasionally with warm water and detergent, but do not overwet. Rinse and allow to dry. Polish, using either a self-shine liquid polish or a wax floor polish.

Wood. A wooden floor should be swept regularly. Wash with warm water and detergent. A thin wax polish will "seal" a wooden floor, giving a non-slip shine. Use a liquid floor polish occasionally to keep the surface in good condition.

Think and Do

1. Give advice on how to care for a new fitted carpet.
2. Design a pattern for a new type of vinyl floor tile.
3. Copy the following diagram into your notebook and write a suitable sentence in each of the boxes.

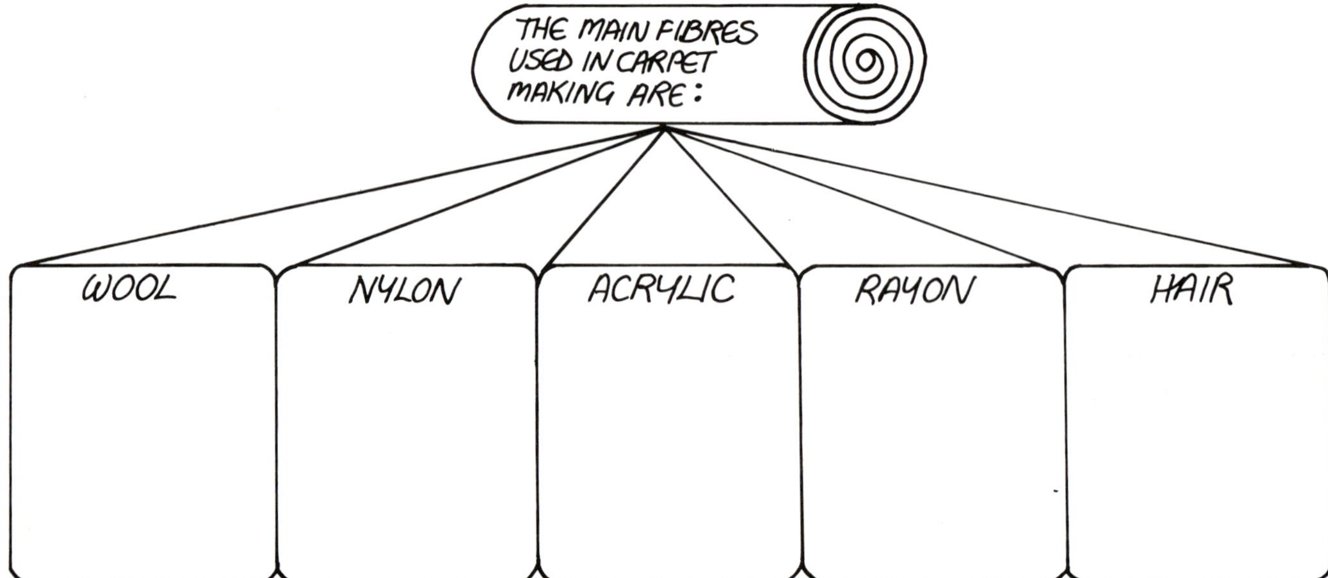

4. Collect pictures of floor coverings and stick them into your notebook. Underneath each picture list the advantages and disadvantages of the floor covering illustrated.

5. Write a paragraph about each of the following:
a. carpet sweepers;
b. vacuum cleaners;
c. electric floor polishers.
6. The following are types of carpets. Name them.

a. LNOWTI ***d.*** MTIRAXSEN
b. UFETDT ***e.*** ARHI
c. LCCIYRA ***f.*** EDNODB

7. Visit a carpet showroom and find out all you can on the following:
a. carpet widths;
b. how carpets are laid;
c. underlays.
8. Suggest a suitable floor covering for each of the following rooms:
a. a kitchen;
b. a lounge/dining area;
c. a young child's bedroom;
d. a bathroom.
9. Are these sentences ***true*** or ***false***?
a. A fitted carpet makes a room look smaller.
b. A Wilton carpet is woven on a loom.
c. A bonded carpet is water-repellent.
d. Cushioned vinyl should be used with a separate underlay.
e. Inlaid linoleum is cheaper than patterned linoleum.
f. New carpets should be vacuumed lightly once or twice a week.
10. Say how you would:
a. seal a wooden floor;
b. remove a tea stain from a tufted carpet;
c. ensure even wear in a carpet square.

Soft furnishings

The term "soft furnishings" refers to the accessories (extras) in a room, such as curtains, cushions, chair covers, bed linen and table linen. It is items like these that add comfort as well as decoration, and help to make a room look homely and inviting. A bare window looks cold and cheerless, and chairs that are faded and worn can have a depressing effect. A clever housewife will add colour, gaiety and warmth by choosing sensible and cheerful soft furnishings. Old furniture can be given a new lease of life with bright covers and gay scatter cushions. Dark rooms can be made lighter and small rooms can be made to look bigger by the right kind of curtains. Look at the two rooms pictured below. Room A looks cold and cheerless. Room B has the same furniture as Room A but looks entirely different. It looks homely and "lived in", and has a welcoming atmosphere. What has caused this change?

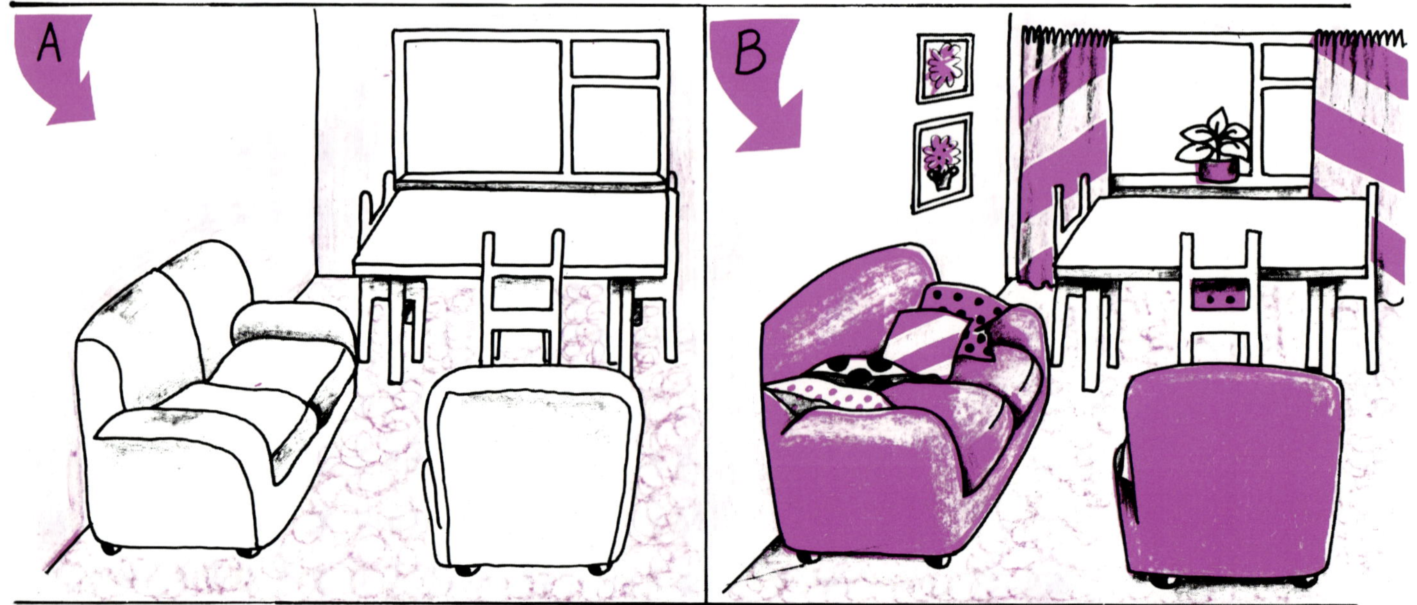

Curtains

When buying curtain material, it is a good idea to know exactly what type and colour you want before starting to look around the shops. If you do not set yourself simple guidelines, you may find that you have chosen material that is completely wrong for the room you are furnishing. Consider the carpet and the furniture in the room. If you have a plain coloured carpet or floor covering, then a patterned curtain material will look effective, but if you have a heavily-patterned floor covering, plain curtains will be safer. Too many patterned areas can make a room look confused and cluttered.

When you have decided on whether you want plain or patterned curtaining, then try to limit the colours that you will consider. It is a good idea to link or contrast the colour of the curtaining with the other colours in the room. It is obvious that some colours do not go well together, while other colours blend or harmonize effectively. The impression that you want to create will depend upon the particular room that you are furnishing. A living room should be warm and inviting, whereas the colour scheme for a bedroom should be cooler and more restful. A large room could be furnished attractively in dark and sombre colours, but a small room needs lighter colours to give the impression of more space. Remember that red, orange and brown are warm colours, and blue, yellow and green are cool colours.

It is important to choose a material that will "hang" or drape well. When buying curtain material always ask to see the material in a hanging position. This will show you whether the material will drape well when hanging at a window. Check that the material will wash well. You will need to know if the colours are fast, and if the material has been pre-shrunk. The shop assistant should be able to tell you this.

It is a good idea, when buying curtaining, to gently squeeze a corner of the material. If the material creases easily or goes limp, then be careful. These are signs that the material is not crease resistant and that the "body" of the material could disappear with washing.

How to measure for curtains

Have a good look at the window that you wish to curtain, and decide what length of curtain will look best. It is sometimes possible to alter the appearance of a window by the clever use of curtaining. Bad features can be disguised and good ones enhanced. The diagrams show identically narrow windows. In Fig. A the curtains have been extended to show the maximum area of glass, and this gives the impression of a larger window than in Fig. B. In Figs. C and D we can see how the use of long and short curtains can alter identical windows.

Long curtains can help to exclude draughts from badly-fitting window frames, and they can improve small windows. Avoid hanging long curtains over central heating radiators. The long curtains will prevent the heat from the radiators warming the room, and the curtains will eventually be damaged by continually touching the hot metal.

When you have decided on the length of curtains that you want, then you will have to measure how much material you will need. Always remember that the more material you use, the "fuller" the curtain will hang. A skimpy curtain does not look as effective as a curtain with lots of folds.

An ordinary gathered curtain should be at least one and a half times the width of the curtain track. It is a good idea, too, to make the curtain track a little wider than the window so that curtains can be drawn well back. If the length of the curtain track A is 200cm, then the curtains will need to be at least one and a half times this width, i.e. 300cm. If the material is 115cm wide, then three widths will give 345cm which is over one and a half times the length of A.

For the different pleated effects, allow extra width. Pinch pleating requires double the width of the curtain track, and some fuller pleated headings require up to three times the width of the track.

When you have worked out the number of widths of material that you require, then you must measure the length. Measure from the bottom of the curtain track to the window sill (for short curtains), or to the floor (for long curtains). Remember that you must add to this length, ***for each curtain***:

- ***a*** at least 8cm for a hem;
- ***b*** twice the height of the heading of the curtain;
- ***c*** extra material for matching a pattern;
- ***d*** about 8cm to allow for shrinkage (not necessary in pre-shrunk materials).

A word about tracks

Curtain tracks can be covered by a pelmet, be unobtrusive or be a bold decorative feature of the curtains. There are many different types available and it is a good idea to have a look at each type before deciding on the one you want.

Curtains are usually clipped or slotted on to tracks by hooks. These metal, plastic or nylon hooks are threaded on to curtain tape, which is attached to the top of each curtain. The curtain tape can be drawn up by special cords to the required width of the window.

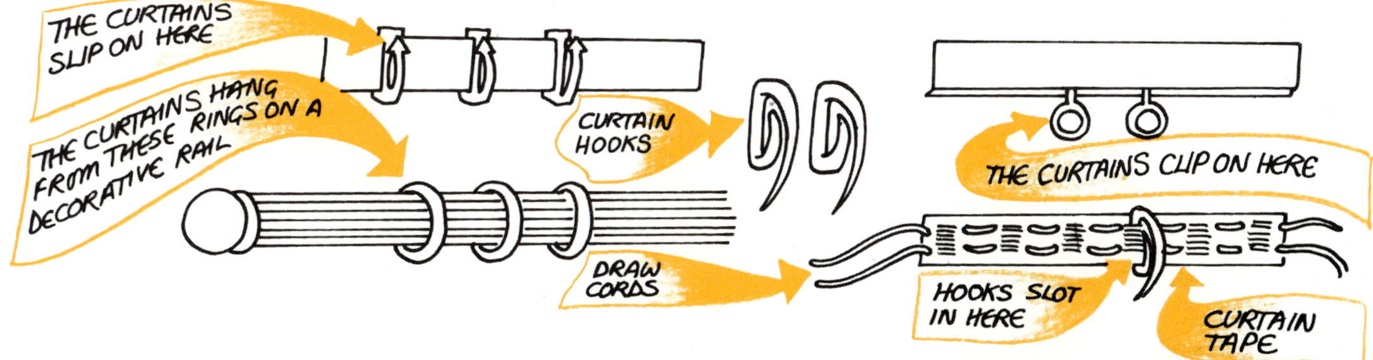

Making curtains

1 Cut the lengths of material needed, remembering to match the pattern and to allow extra material for the hem and heading of each curtain.

2 Snip down the selvedge edges of each curtain at 8cm intervals. This will help the edges to stay flat.

3 Join widths where necessary by pinning and tacking the right sides together. Allow a 1·5cm seam. Sew with a loose stitch. Press seam open.

4 Make side hems of about 3cm width. Pin and tack into position. Either slip stitch or machine loosely.

5 For an ordinary heading, turn down 3cm at the top of each curtain and pin the curtain tape 1·5cm from the top. Machine the tape into place, leaving the draw cord free at one end. If you are making an elaborate heading, follow the instructions given with the special hooks and tape.

6 Pull the draw cord to the width of the window and tie.

7 Attach the curtains to the curtain track and leave to hang for a day.

8 Turn up the hem and slip stitch into position.

Curtain linings

Most curtains are improved by the addition of a lining. Some very heavy materials drape better if they are left unlined but usually a lining gives body to curtains and also protects the colours from the fading effect of the sunlight. Check that the lining material being used has been pre-shrunk. A lining should be made in the same way as the curtain. It can either be left to hang freely or it can be attached to the curtain by slip stitching. A loose lining is easier to wash and iron, but does not hang as tidily at the window.

Ready-made curtains

Some curtains can be bought ready-made. They are available in a variety of colours, materials and sizes and will fit most normal windows. They are more expensive to buy than curtain material but are expertly made and usually of a high quality. Ready-made curtains can be bought lined or unlined. Can you think of any advantages and disadvantages of buying ready-made curtains?

Blinds

Window blinds are an alternative to curtains or can be used as well. They can be bought in plain colours or in a variety of attractive patterns. Each blind is made to fit a particular window, and any size or shape can be ordered. All blinds are either washable or can be sponged clean with a damp cloth. There are two main types of blind:

a venetian;
b roller.

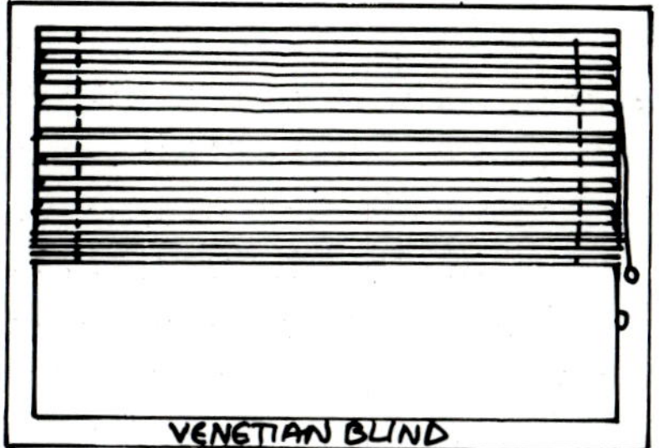

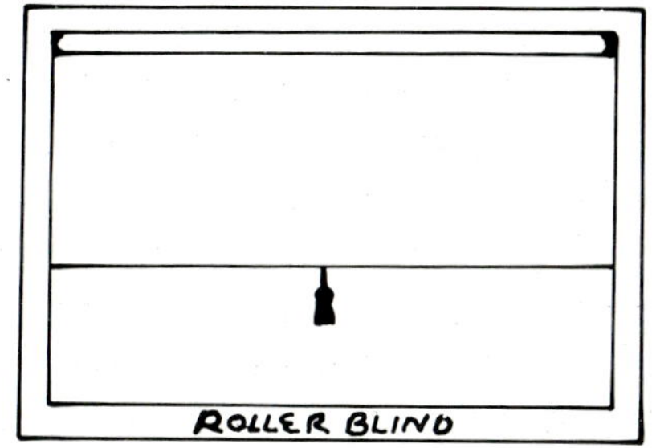

A ***venetian blind*** is hard-wearing. It is made of horizontal aluminium or plastic strips which can be lifted or dropped when necessary. The strips or slats can be set to a slanting position that will allow light to pass through but will also give maximum privacy. A venetian blind can be obtained in a variety of plain colours that will blend in with most furnishing schemes. It is expensive to buy but will last for many years. A less expensive type of venetian blind is the slatted roll-up blind. This is made of strips of vinyl which will roll up to any position but cannot be tilted.

A ***roller blind*** can be made from any good-quality curtaining fabric that has been specially stiffened, or it can be made from vinyl. Material can be chosen that will link up with the other soft furnishings in the room. A roller blind works on a spring system, the fabric wrapping around a top wooden pole. It can be pulled down to hold at any position. A roller blind is less expensive to buy than a venetian blind but it is not as durable. Do-it-yourself blind kits can be bought. These come complete with instructions and all the fittings necessary.

Cushion covers

Cushions can be a striking feature of a room. As well as being useful to lean against, they can brighten a room and add charm and colour. Cushion pads and covers can be bought or made in a variety of shapes. They can be plain in colour and decorated with fringing, piping cord or buttons, or they can be made from patterned material.

When choosing either ready-made cushion covers or material to make your own, look for a good-quality fabric. It is sometimes a good idea to use the same material as for the curtains. This can link up different areas of the room and looks effective. The material should be hard-wearing, washable and, if possible, crease resistant.

Chair covers

It is sad and extravagant to abandon a comfortable chair just because the cover looks worn or faded. Covers can be bought or made that can give extra life to any seating unit. A strong pre-shrunk material should be used, and it is important to buy material that will wash well. If you wish to recover a chair, settee or seating unit, it is a good idea to attend an evening class on soft furnishings, and seek help. It is important to obtain a professional finish with the fitting and making of the covers and this takes time and skill.

An alternative to this, is to buy ready-made stretch covers. These can be bought in a variety of colours and shapes. They are hard-wearing and easy to launder. Stretch covers are not cheap to buy but it is often worth considering this rather than having the expense of buying new furniture.

Sheets and pillowcases

Sheets can be bought separately, in pairs or in sets with matching pillowcases. Do choose the right-sized sheets for the bed you are covering.

Type of bed	Size of bed	Size of cotton sheets	Size of mixture sheets
Small single	90cm × 190cm	175cm × 255cm 175cm × 275cm 200cm × 255cm 200cm × 275cm	175cm × 260cm
Standard single	100cm × 200cm	175cm × 275cm 200cm × 275cm	175cm × 260cm
Small double	135cm × 190cm	230cm × 255cm 230cm × 275cm	230cm × 260cm
Standard double	150cm × 200cm	230cm × 275cm	230cm × 260cm

Sheets can be white or coloured, plain or patterned, and they are made in a variety of fabrics. The most popular fibres used are:

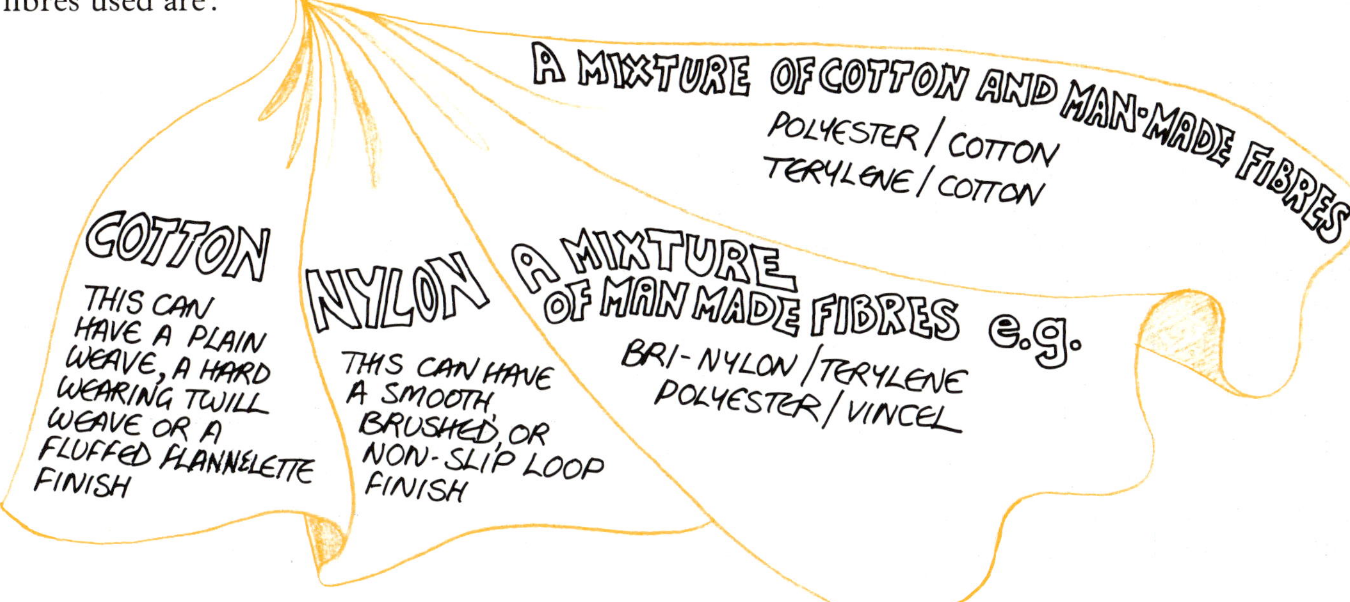

Cotton sheets are cool, comfortable and hard-wearing, but they are expensive to buy. Flannelette sheets have extra warmth for winter wear. Nylon sheets are very hard-wearing. They are easy to wash and dry, and do not require ironing. Nylon sheets are cheaper to buy than cotton or mixed fibre sheets. Cotton mixture sheets have the coolness and comfort of cotton, plus the hard-wearing easy-to-launder properties of man-made fibres.

Sheets can be fully-fitted, semi-fitted or flat. Fully-fitted bottom sheets hug the mattress and stay flat during use. This saves time and energy when making the bed. Semi-fitted top sheets have two mitred corners and two flat corners. Flat sheets can be tucked under the mattress and have the advantage of being interchangeable, e.g. a lightly-soiled top sheet can be used again as a bottom sheet when the bed linen is changed.

Pillowcases can have a frilled or plain edge. A plain edged pillowcase is called a "housewife" style pillowcase. The standard pillowcase size is 50cm × 75cm.

Blankets

The most popular fibres used for blankets are:

When buying blankets buy the best that you can afford. Choose ones that are easy to launder. Most blankets can be machine-washed and drip-dried. It is a good idea to look for blankets that are also mothproofed and shrink-resistant. Blankets can be bought in a variety of rich colours. The ends can be hemmed or bound. The open weave of cellular blankets traps air and this helps to give added warmth and insulation. Do choose the right-sized blanket for the bed you are covering.

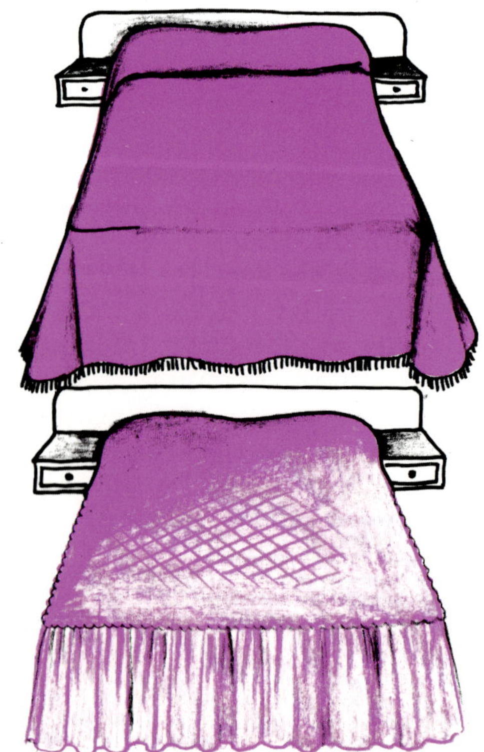

Type of bed	Size of bed	Size of blanket
Small single	90cm × 190cm	180cm × 240cm
Standard single	100cm × 200cm	200cm × 250cm
Small double	135cm × 190cm	230cm × 250cm
Standard double	150cm × 200cm	260cm × 250cm

Bedspreads

Bedspreads can be used to cover beds during the daytime. Bedspreads can be bought in a variety of colours and fabrics. They can be flat or fitted.

The most popular fibres used for bedspreads are:

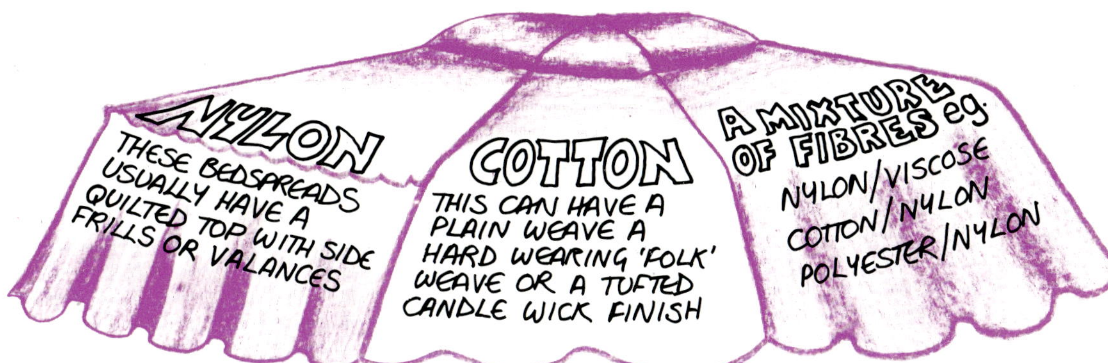

A good bedspread will:

a look attractive;
b be hard-wearing;
c be easy to launder.

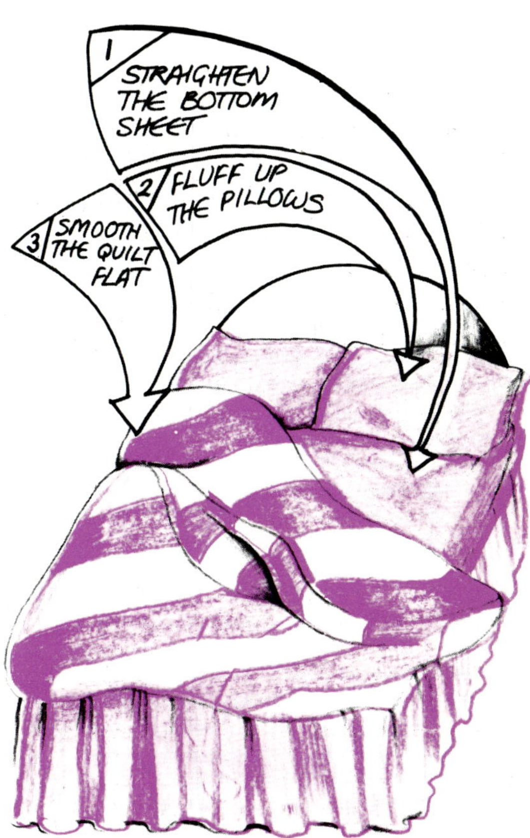

Continental-style quilts

A continental-style quilt can be used as an alternative to sheets and blankets. This type of quilt consists of a big bag which is divided into sections. The sections are filled with feathers, down or terylene. The quilt is protected by a cover, which can be removed for washing. A continental-style quilt should be large enough to drape over the edges of the bed. This provides maximum insulation for the body, keeping it warm in winter and cool in summer. Bed-making is easier with a continental-style quilt.

It is possible to buy co-ordinating (matching) sheets, valances, pillowcases and quilt covers, in a variety of colours, patterns and easy-care fabrics.

Pillows

Always buy the best pillows that you can afford. A good pillow will retain its shape during use and be soft and resilient, but a cheap pillow may lose its shape, becoming hard and lumpy.

The most common fillings for a pillow are:

Electric blankets

There are two types of electric blanket:

a an overblanket;
b an underblanket.

An ***overblanket*** usually has a thermostatic control which can be set to a required temperature. An overblanket can be used instead of ordinary blankets and should be left switched on throughout the night.

An ***underblanket*** can be used to pre-heat a bed to either a single heat or a thermostatically-set heat. An underblanket should ***not*** be left switched on throughout the night.

Most electric blankets can be washed but do read the manufacturer's instructions carefully. Always check that an electric blanket has been approved by the B.E.A.B. (see page 154).

Towels

Most towels are made of cotton and can be bought in a variety of colours and patterns. Good quality towels will:

a feel soft and springy;
b be absorbent;
c wash easily.

It is wise to wash deep-coloured towels separately until you are sure that the colour does not "run". Hand towels are suitable for normal use but the larger bath towels are better for having a bath or going swimming. Paper towels are hygienic and useful to have in the kitchen.

Tea towels

Pure linen tea towels are very hard-wearing. They dry and polish efficiently but they are expensive to buy. For this reason most tea towels are made of cotton. These can have a flat weave or a "terry towelling" finish. Always choose a good-sized tea towel. Small, skimpy tea towels are often of an inferior quality and may not wash or wear well.

Table linen

Tablecloths can be bought in a variety of colours, patterns and easy care fabrics. The most popular fabrics for tablecloths are: ▶

When buying table linen do check that all colours are fast and that the material is shrink-resistant. A busy housewife may also want to choose fabrics that can be drip-dried with a non-iron finish. Cotton damask cloths require starching but their crisp, clean appearance looks lovely for that special occasion meal. Tablecloths can be bought in square, oblong or circular shapes, and are sometimes sold in sets with matching napkins.

Individual place mats can look very attractive on a formica or wooden-topped table. Place mats can be made from woven grasses, vinyl-coated fabrics, cotton, etc.

The care and cleaning of soft furnishings

Curtains

Brush into the folds of curtains once a week, or clean with the upholstery nozzle on a vacuum. When curtains require cleaning, take them down and remove the curtain hooks. Untie the draw strings of the curtain tape and pull the curtains out flat. It is important to know from what material the curtains are made, as this will affect the type of cleaning.

Very heavy brocades, velvets and velours should be dry cleaned. It is often easier to have heavily-lined curtains dry cleaned also, because their weight can make them difficult to handle. Curtains that have a detachable lining can be laundered at home.

Here are some points to help you when washing curtains:

1 Most modern fabrics can be machine washed, but it is a good idea to soak in cold, salt water before the first wash. This helps to stabilize loose dyes and minimize shrinkage.

2 Rinse.

3 Give a short wash in warm water with a mild detergent.

4 Rinse well in cold water.

5 Spin for a short time or drip-dry.

6 Use a hot iron for cotton and linen fabrics, and a cool iron for man-made fabrics. It is a good idea to check with the washing instructions for the particular material you are treating. Some modern fibres do not need ironing and any creases noticeable after drip-drying, will fall out when the curtains are hanging. When ironing lined curtains, iron the lining first.

Glass fibre curtains should be hand washed in warm water. Do not squeeze or rub the material. Rinse well in warm water. Drip-dry. This fabric will not require ironing and will dry quickly.

Mixtures of cotton/rayon and cotton/acetate should be given a minimum wash. Unless these materials have been pre-shrunk they will shrink during washing.

Net curtains should be hand washed in warm water. After rinsing they should be drip-dried. Discoloured nylon and terylene net curtains can be "whitened" by a special dye.

Blinds

The slats of venetian blinds can be wiped clean with a damp cloth and any liquid detergent. A special pair of "tongs" can be bought that will fit into the slats and clean two or three of them at once. Venetian blinds can be cleaned while they are in a hanging position. Roller blinds should be lifted down and opened flat before cleaning. They can be sponged over lightly with a damp cloth and a liquid detergent. Do not wet the blind too much. Allow to dry before replacing at the window.

Cushion covers

Most cushion covers can be machine washed. Give a minimum wash in hand hot water with a mild detergent. Be careful with dark and deep colours because the dyes may not be fast. Care should be taken with decorative finishes such as fringing and piping cord. Many ready-made cushion covers will drip-dry and do not require any ironing.

Chair covers

Fitted chair covers are usually made from strong cotton or linen materials, and will wash well. Machine-wash and spin or drip-dry. Iron all seams on the wrong side with a hot iron, and then turn the covers over and iron on the right side. Air well before replacing the covers on the chairs. Nylon stretch covers are hard-wearing. They are easy to wash and drip-dry, and do not require ironing.

Sheets and Pillowcases

Sheets and pillowcases can be machine washed and the H.L.C.C. label should be checked for details of the correct washing procedure for each type of fabric. Some sheets and pillowcases may require little or no ironing. Always treat dark and deep-coloured sheets and pillowcases with care until you are certain that the colours do not "run".

Blankets

It is advisable to take very heavy or bulky blankets to the launderette where the large-sized washing machines and tumble dryers can cope with them efficiently. Heavy blankets may also be dry cleaned. Medium or lightweight blankets can be washed by hand (preferably in the bath), or machine washed. Always rinse thoroughly before spin drying or wringing. Blankets should be pulled gently into shape when hanging on the line. Always air blankets well.

Bedspreads

Most bedspreads can be machine washed but do check the washing instructions given. Take care with decorative finishes such as fringing, piping, frills and valances. Many bedspreads will drip-dry and have a non-iron finish.

Continental-style quilts

If a quilt is protected with a cover, cleaning should not be necessary, but down and feather-filled quilts can be dry cleaned or returned to the manufacturer for cleaning, if badly soiled. Terylene-filled quilts can be machine washed but it is advisable to take them to a launderette and use the larger-sized machines and tumble dryers.

Pillows

Feather and down-filled pillows can be dry cleaned but do allow time for any fumes to disappear before re-using. It is a good idea to hang them on the clothes line on a dry, windy day. Terylene-filled pillows can be dry cleaned, though some types can be machine washed. Do check with the cleaning instructions. Foam rubber-filled pillows can be sponged clean but should not be wet through.

Electric blankets

Always check the manufacturer's instructions carefully before attempting to clean an electric blanket.

Towels and tea towels

Heavily-soiled towels will wash easily if they are given a pre-wash soak. Do be certain though, that all colours are "fast". White cottons and linens can be given a maximum wash in very hot water, and can be boiled if necessary. (Boiling sterilizes and helps to keep clothes a good colour.) Coloured cottons and linens, whose colours are fast, can be given a maximum wash in hot water. Always rinse towels thoroughly before drying. A fabric conditioner in the final rinse will keep towels soft and springy. White towels can be bleached if necessary.

Table linen

Table linen should be washed according to the instructions given, so do check with the H.L.C.C. label. Always see that stains are removed quickly. Remember that:

- ***a*** a seersucker finish does not need ironing;
- ***b*** many cotton, nylon and terylene cloths have a drip-dry, non-iron finish;
- ***c*** cotton damask cloths should be starched to give a crisp, clean appearance;
- ***d*** vinyl-coated and plastic materials need only be wiped over with a damp cloth.

Think and Do

1. What type of window covering would you recommend for each of the following rooms? Give a reason for your choice.

a. A bathroom.
b. A small, dark living room.
c. A child's bedroom.
d. A kitchen.

2. Collect as many different scraps of curtaining material as you can find. Cut them into 10cm squares and stick them neatly into your notebook. Under each one write ***a.*** the type of material and ***b.*** how it should be laundered.

3. Find out the current prices for each of the following:
a. ordinary curtain tape;
b. a continental-style quilt suitable for a double bed;
c. foam rubber cushion pads;
d. a good quality bath towel;
e. venetian blinds;
f. a large nylon seersucker tablecloth;
g. an electric underblanket.

4. Imagine that you are choosing the soft furnishings for a new home. How would you:
a. make a cold room appear warmer;
b. make a large room cosier;
c. make a small window seem larger;
d. make a dark room lighter?

5. Imagine that you have been asked to promote a "Buy a continental quilt" week! Design a poster for it.

6. How would you:
a. launder a cotton tea towel;
b. choose material for some bedroom curtains;
c. clean a venetian blind?

7. Look through some magazines and find pictures of bed linen that you like. Stick them into your notebook under the heading "Let's brighten our bedrooms".

8. Imagine that you have been given some plain navy blue cotton material. Design a cushion cover suitable for a lounge chair. Say what trimmings you would use.

9. Measure one of the windows in your home. Work out how much material you would need if you wished to make a pair of short curtains with an ordinary heading.

10. Copy out this crossword and complete it.

Clues across
1. A type of blind.
2. Can be used to decorate a cushion cover.
3. Curtains are hung from these.

Clues down
4. A type of chair cover.
5. A warm colour.
6. This will protect curtains from the sunlight.

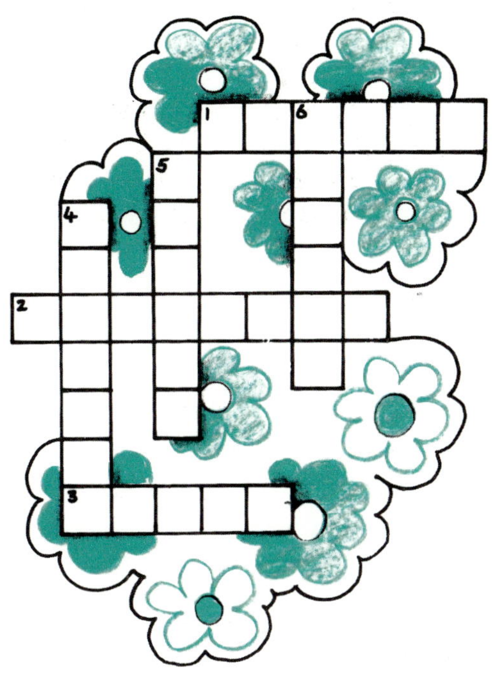

Furniture and fittings

In this chapter we will learn how to choose furniture and fittings for a home.

Styles of furniture

Furniture can be loosely divided into two groups:

a traditional;
b modern.

The term ***traditional*** is used to describe the various styles of furniture that were popular many years ago. Furniture that is old (antique) can be very expensive to buy, but it is possible to buy good reproductions (copies) of the original styles. These are much cheaper to buy, and are machine-made instead of being made by hand.

Here are some examples of traditional furniture.

The term ***modern*** is used to describe the style of furniture that is popular today. It is simple in design and does not have the ornate carvings and decorative features of traditional furniture. Modern furniture is usually machine-made, though there are some do-it-yourself enthusiasts who produce hand-made furniture.

Here are some examples of modern furniture.

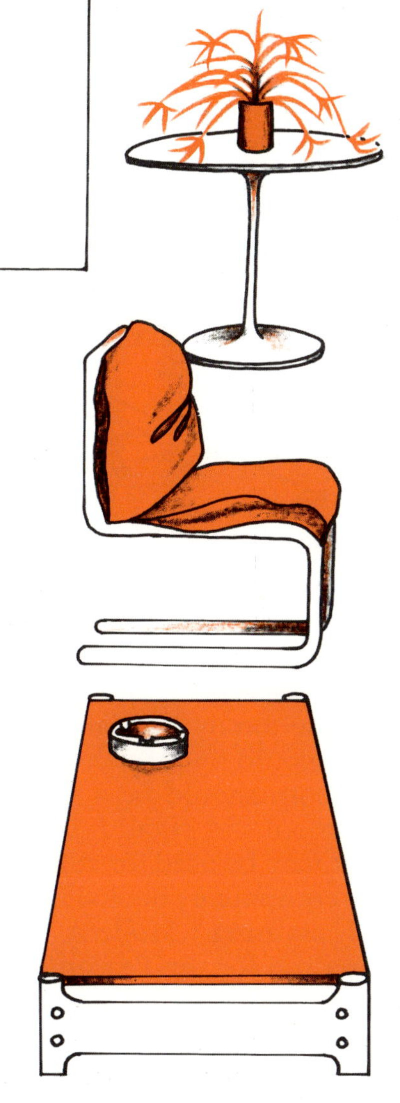

Good design in furniture

A well-designed piece of furniture is both ***functional*** and ***beautiful***. This means that it will do the job of work it is intended to do, and will also look pleasing to the eye, e.g. a well-designed chair should be comfortable to sit upon, as well as being a lovely piece of furniture. A chair that looks lovely but is very uncomfortable, is ***not*** well designed.

When choosing a piece of furniture always ask yourself the following questions.

1 Will it be functional and practical?

2 Does it look attractive? Remember that fashions change quickly. It is often more sensible to choose a simpler style than a "way-out" style that will quickly date.

3 Does it seem well-made and of good materials?

4 Will it be durable?

5 Can it be easily cleaned? There should not be any unnecessary ornaments and carvings to collect dust.

6 Is it in the right price range?

If you can answer "yes" to these questions, then you will be buying a well-designed piece of furniture. Do try to make up your own mind. Choosing furniture is a very personal matter. Do not be swayed by tempting advertisements in magazines, brochures and on television. Decide whether each piece of furniture suits ***you***, ***your family*** and the ***type of life you lead***.

Acquiring furniture

Most people cannot afford to completely furnish a home when they are first married. They may choose to:

Choosing bedroom furniture

A bedroom is usually only used when dressing and sleeping, but occasionally it can also double as a study, workroom, homework area or children's playroom, depending on the needs of the family. When such a dual role is necessary a bedroom should be furnished with this in mind.

A bedroom should be a well-ventilated, light and comfortable room. It should have plenty of storage space, because it may be used for storing spare bed linen, suitcases, sporting equipment, books, hobbies, games, etc. as well as personal clothing. Modern homes tend to have small bedrooms and for this reason it is often a good idea to have built-in cupboards along one wall. This type of arrangement provides good storage space and uses less floor space than a traditional free-standing bedroom suite. Extra units can be added when necessary, the cupboards being extended upwards towards the ceiling, thus avoiding the waste of space which could become a dust trap.

A built-in storage unit can provide:

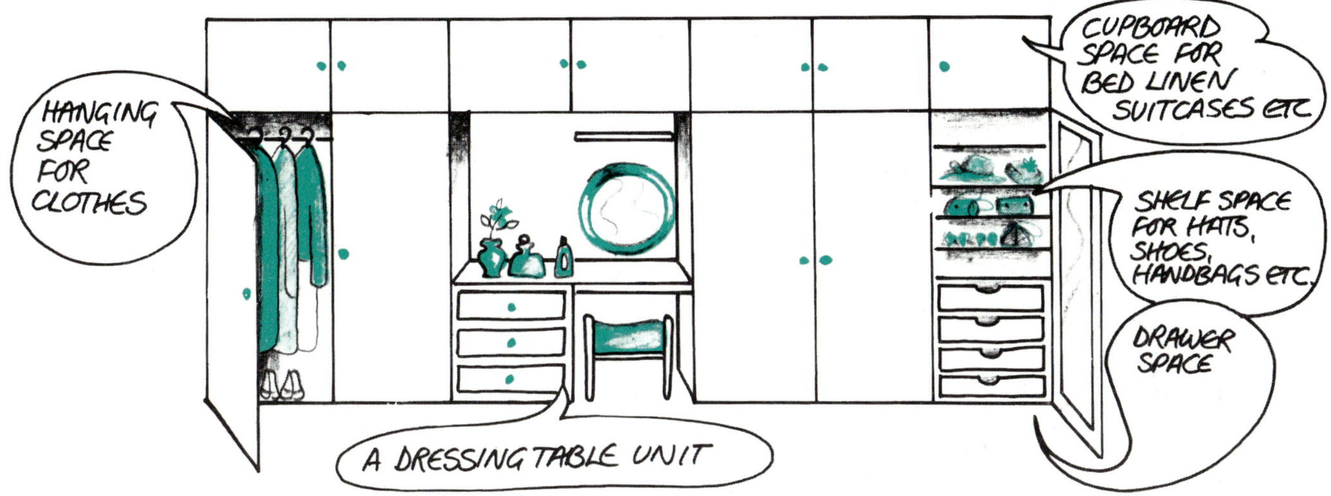

A bedroom suite usually consists of:

Each piece of furniture is free-standing and can be arranged to suit the shape of the bedroom. In this way alcoves, window and chimney recesses can be used to advantage.

Where storage space in a bedroom is limited, it is a good idea to consider buying:

a an ottoman or blanket chest;

b a pull-out or sliding drawer unit that will fit under the bed;

c a cabin trunk (very useful for storing toys, games, out-of-season clothes);
d an extra chest of drawers.

A bed is an expensive piece of furniture and must be chosen with care. A good bed should:

a be comfortable;
b give support to the spine;
c be long and wide enough to allow ease of movement;
d be hard-wearing;
e be movable (do check that it is on castors).

A modern bed consists of a base and a mattress. The base can have a firm or soft edge. A firm-edged divan base has a wooden frame which surrounds the springs. This gives a harder base which will wear well. A soft-edged divan base, which has springing right to the edge of the base, has a more luxurious feel but does not wear as well as a firm-edged divan base. The mattress can have a quilted decorative finish which is easily cleaned, or a deep buttoned effect. Do check that the mattress cover or "ticking" is made from a hard-wearing material. A mattress can have a spring interior or a plastic/rubber foam filling. It is a good idea to lie down on each type of mattress in turn before deciding which kind gives you the support and comfort you need.

A separate bedhead or headboard can be bought if required. A well-designed bedhead will give support when sitting up in bed and will act as a protective covering for the wall. It should be made from a hard-wearing material that can be easily cleaned. Bedside tables, cabinets and shelves can be fitted to the bedhead or be free-standing at the side of the bed.

A bed can be single or double sized.

A small single bed	90cm × 190cm
A standard single bed	100cm × 200cm
A small double bed	135cm × 190cm
A standard double bed	150cm × 200cm

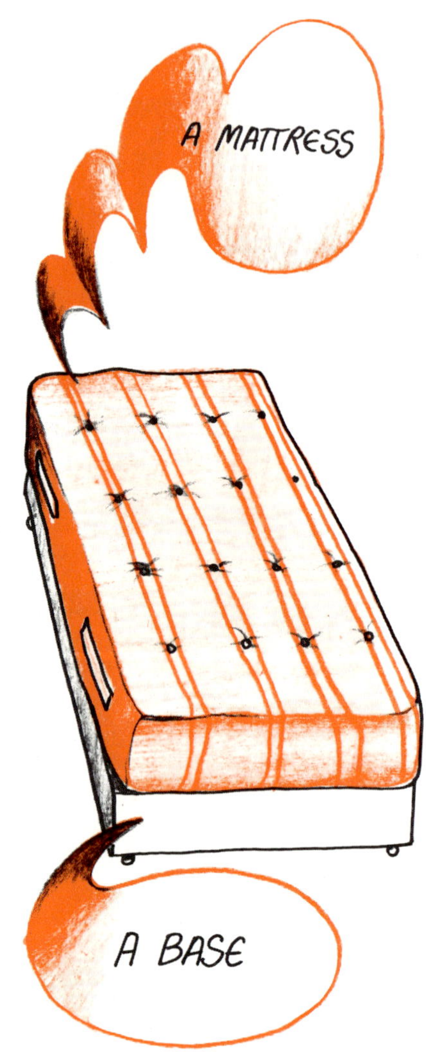

It is possible to buy sofa beds, sliding beds that store one on top of the other and folding beds. These will quickly convert to accommodate the extra overnight guest. Bunk beds (75cm × 190cm) can provide sleeping space for two people without using extra floor space, and are a good idea especially for young children. Remember that continental-style quilts can make bunk bed-making easier.

Choosing lounge/dining room furniture

You may wish to furnish your living/dining area with traditional furniture or you may wish to use modern, sectional furniture with built-in wall storage units. For this reason it is a good idea to plan a furnishing scheme before beginning to acquire individual items of furniture.

A living area requires seating accommodation. This can be in the form of:

The type of seating accommodation that is chosen will depend upon personal preference and the life style of the family concerned.

When choosing seating accommodation ask yourself the following questions.

1 Is it comfortable? A chair back should follow the curve of the spine, and a whole chair should attempt to copy the shape of the human body when in a sitting position. Avoid seats that have hard ridges, prominent buttons, and arms that are too high or too low.

2 Will it be durable? Choose seats that are made from or covered with a hard-wearing material. This is particularly important where there are young children and/or household pets.
3 Can it be easily cleaned? Many modern upholstering materials can be wiped or sponged clean. This is an advantage especially where there are children. Remember that dark colours do not become dirty as quickly as light colours, and that patterned or textured fabrics do not show stains as readily as plain ones. Reversible cushions, loose slip-on or zipped covers for ease of cleaning, are all sensible features worth considering when buying seating accommodation.

A living area requires storage accommodation for such things as hobbies, books, games, records, magazines, etc. A combined living/dining area will need storage space for crockery, cutlery and table linen also. There are many different types of storage unit available for living/dining areas and a suitable combination can be picked from those listed in the diagram.

It is possible to buy space-saving wall units that combine some or all of these storage and display features. The illustration below shows a wall storage unit that would be suitable for a living/dining area. It is compact, space-saving and can be bought in a variety of easy-care finishes. Extra units can be added when necessary.

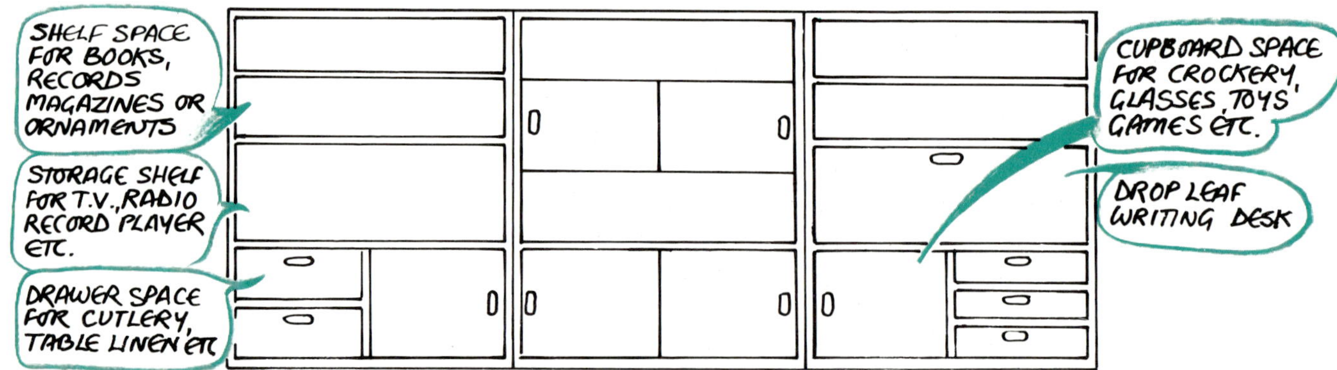

Dining tables and chairs are available in a variety of styles and can be made from wood, hard-wearing laminated plastic or glass with chromium steel supports. Tables can be square, oblong, round or oval, and many can be extended by the use of a drop leaf or a central panel that slots or swivels into position. Matching chairs can be bought separately, in pairs or as part of a suite. Do look for comfortable, sturdy chairs that can be easily cleaned. Be wary of chairs that have awkward ledges. These can collect dust and food particles and will be difficult to keep clean.

Choosing china, glassware and cutlery

Choosing china, glassware and cutlery can be difficult because there are so many styles and patterns available. Here are a few general points to help you.

1 Do consider having some "everyday" tableware as well as a "good" dinner and tea service. This will help to prolong the life of your best items.

2 It is a good idea to buy matching dinner and tea services. This means that pieces can be interchanged, a useful point to consider when camouflaging breakages.

3 Always choose a pattern of tableware that can be bought as individual items. In this way pieces can be bought when you can afford them, and breakages can be replaced. Do check that you are not buying a discontinued line and that the pattern is likely to be produced for a number of years.

4 When choosing glassware, hold the items gently in your hand. They should feel to be balanced. Some glasses are flimsy around the base and can be easily knocked over. Choose a design that can be bought separately, so that sets can be built up gradually and breakages replaced.

5 Cutlery can be bought as individual items, as place settings or as a canteen. Stainless steel cutlery is very popular because it is easy to keep clean and can be bought in a variety of attractive designs. Cutlery can have stainless steel, plastic or wooden handles. Always check any special washing instructions that may apply to the cutlery you choose.

6 Do handle cutlery before buying. Each item should feel balanced. There should not be any clumsy edges or sharp ridges that could cause discomfort. The prongs of forks should not be too close together because this can cause difficulty when washing up.

Light fittings

Adequate artificial lighting is important in a home. It prevents eye-strain and accidents. The type of lighting used in each room may vary. Some areas in a home are used for "close" work, such as reading, writing, cooking, sewing, etc. It is important that these areas are well lit. "Relaxing" areas in a home can be lit by soft, diffused lights.

Electricity is used for most types of artificial lighting. It is easy to control, efficient to use and does not give off any fumes. Places without electricity have to rely on paraffin lamps or camping gas fitments.

An electric light bulb can be made of clear, pearl, opal or coloured glass. It can be "pear" or "mushroom" shaped, or designed to look like a candle. An electric light bulb is filled with an inert gas and has a coiled metal filament of tungsten. An electric light bulb will burn for approximately 1000 hours. Some long-life bulbs can be bought which will burn for up to 5000 hours.

There is a wide range of light fittings available. A light fitting can give:

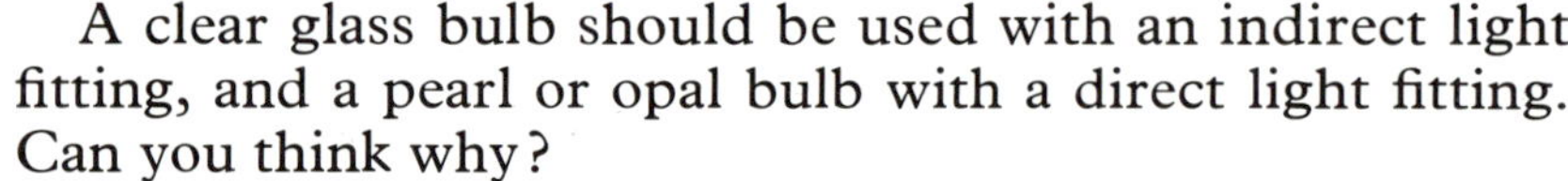

A clear glass bulb should be used with an indirect light fitting, and a pearl or opal bulb with a direct light fitting. Can you think why?

A fluorescent light fitting glows with an all-round light which is shadowless.

Some modern light fittings are shown opposite.

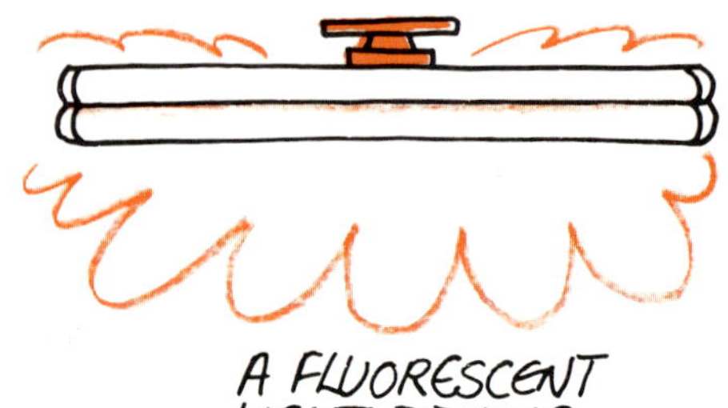

Choosing light fittings

Choose a fitting that will take a 100 or 150 watt bulb for the centre light in a room. Chandelier-type fittings that have

two or three lights are suitable for living/dining rooms, and can be used with a 60 watt bulb in each holder. It is advisable to "spotlight" areas of close work with an extra 60 watt bulb, e.g. table lamp, spotlight, standard lamp. Check that staircases, halls and kitchens are well lit.

Remember that electric light bulbs give off heat. Some types of plastic, fabric and parchment fittings will only take up to a certain wattage of bulb. If this size is exceeded, the fitting will be damaged by the heat from the bulb. Always check that the fitting you choose is suitable for the wattage of bulb you will be using. If in doubt, do ask the shop assistant.

Care and cleaning of glass surfaces and fittings

Glass is used in the home for:

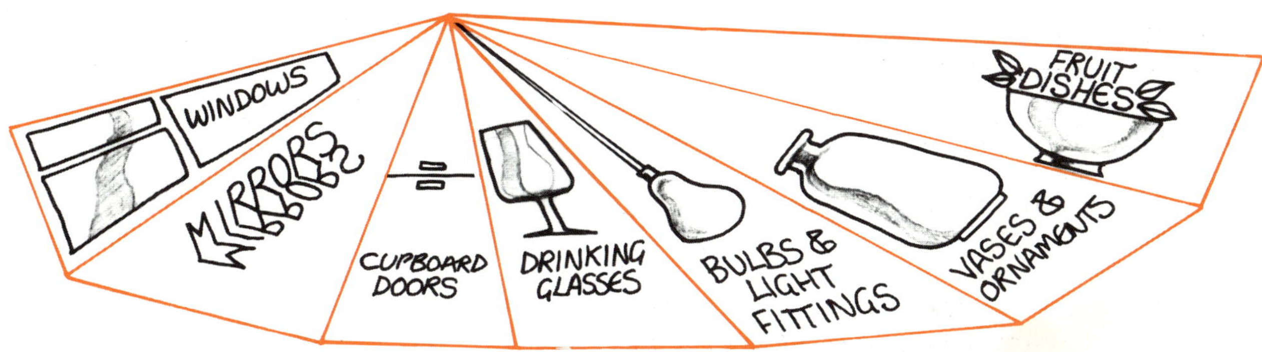

All glass surfaces must be cleaned regularly. Dull mirrors, grey windows and dusty vases have a depressing effect. Glass should always look ***clear*** and ***sparkling***.

Large areas of glass, such as windows, cupboard doors and mirrors, can be cleaned using:

- ***a*** warm water and a detergent;
- ***b*** warm water and a window "leather";
- ***c*** methylated spirits on a damp cloth;
- ***d*** a window cleaning aerosol;
- ***e*** a window cleaning fluid (either in a bottle or a "squeezy" container).

These are all efficient ways of cleaning glass. The modern window cleansers are the quickest to use, but can be expensive if used extravagantly. Always read the instructions on the product.

It is not a good idea to clean windows on a bright, sunny day, as they show up very streaky.

Drinking glasses, fruit dishes, vases and ornaments should be washed in hot, soapy water (not too hot), rinsed well and then dried on a linen or cotton tea towel. A final polish with a dry cloth will give an added sparkle. Do be careful when washing cut-glass dishes, vases, and fragile ornaments. Always handle them gently.

Care and cleaning of wooden surfaces and fittings

Wood is used in the home for:

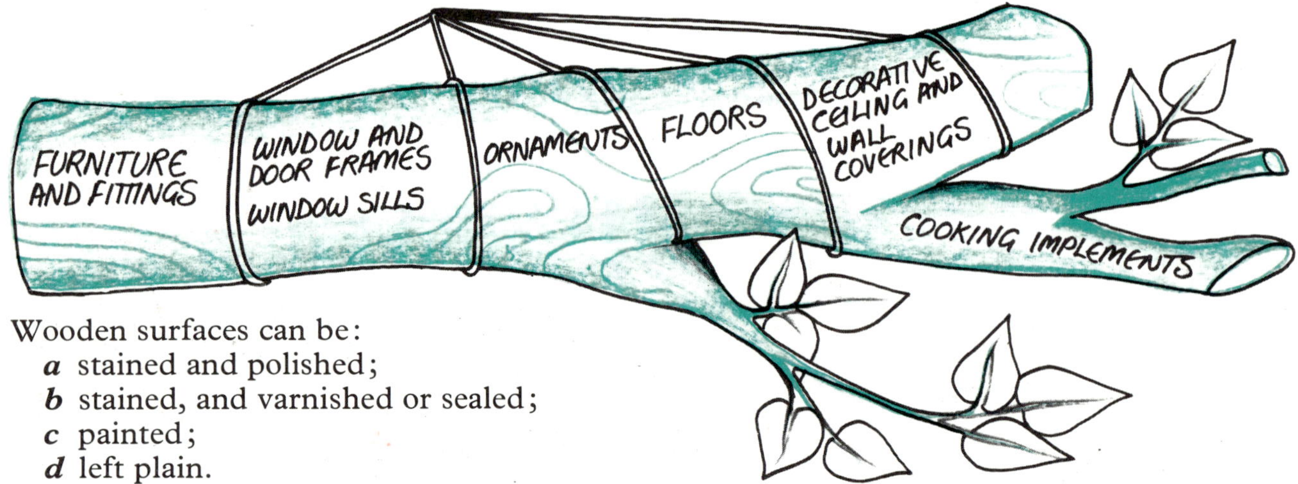

Wooden surfaces can be:

- ***a*** stained and polished;
- ***b*** stained, and varnished or sealed;
- ***c*** painted;
- ***d*** left plain.

Polished wooden surfaces should be dusted frequently with a soft, clean duster. Polished wooden surfaces that have become dirty, can be wiped clean using a damp cloth and a warm water and vinegar solution. Always dry thoroughly with a cloth, before polishing. A wax polish or silicone-based furniture cream can be used to nourish the wood. A self-shine spray polish can also be used. Do check that crevices and ledges are cleaned thoroughly. A soft brush can be used to penetrate awkward corners. Teak furniture does not require polishing. Occasionally an oil or teak preservative can be used to re-vitalize the wood.

Painted wooden surfaces should be dusted frequently. Regular washing with warm water and detergent will freshen the wood and remove dirt. Obstinate stains can be wiped off with a cleansing paste, or rubbed gently with a scouring powder. Always rinse painted wooden surfaces and then rub dry.

Plain wooden surfaces need frequent scrubbing to keep them looking white and clean. Use warm, soapy water and scouring powder (if necessary), and always scrub the way of the grain. Rinse thoroughly and wipe dry.

Decorative wooden coverings for walls and ceilings should be treated with a fire-resistant finish. There are many polyurethane finishes which can be applied to wooden surfaces. These give a shiny, durable, protective coating, and can be dusted clean.

Remember to use ***non-slip polishes*** on wooden floors.

All wooden surfaces can be attacked by ***woodworm***. Do look out for the tell-tale tiny holes and have the wood treated or get rid of the article before it spreads.

Care and cleaning of metal surfaces and fittings

Metal is used in the home for:

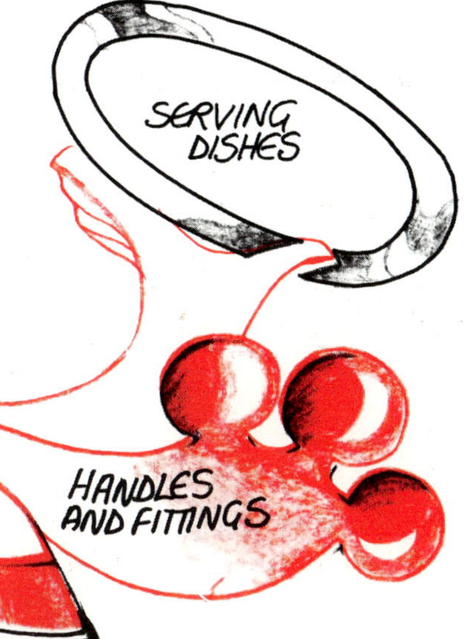

All metal surfaces should be cleaned regularly. Stained, tarnished, rusty and dirty metal surfaces:

- ***a*** look depressing;
- ***b*** are unhygienic;
- ***c*** cannot work efficiently, e.g. a tarnished reflector on a gas or electric fire will not reflect heat.

Metal surfaces can be kept bright and clean by washing in warm water and detergent. They should be rinsed well and dried with a soft cloth.

1 Stains on aluminium and tin surfaces can be removed with a cleansing paste. (Remember to rinse well.)

2 Copper, brass and bronze ornaments can be polished with a special cleaner or impregnated cloth. (Read the instructions carefully.)

3 Stainless steel should be polished with a dry duster, after being washed. (Never use scouring powder.)

4 Chromium handles and decorative features should be polished with a dry duster, after being washed. A special cleaner can be bought if necessary.

5 Cutlery, serving dishes and ornaments made of silver or E.P.N.S. should be cleaned with a special liquid or "dip" polish. A long term cleaner can be used which will keep silver and E.P.N.S. shiny for weeks. (Always wash cutlery and serving dishes in hot water and detergent after cleaning, and then rinse thoroughly before polishing dry.)

6 Non-stick saucepans should be treated with care. They should not be scratched or scoured. Stains should be soaked off, and the saucepans washed in warm water and detergent, using a soft cloth or sponge.

Care and cleaning of laminated plastic surfaces

Laminated plastic (e.g. Formica, Melamine) is used in the home for:

A laminated plastic surface is hard-wearing, and easy to clean. It makes an excellent working surface in kitchens, bathrooms and children's playrooms. This type of surface should be washed with warm water and detergent, rinsed and wiped dry. Stains can be removed with a cleansing paste.

Care and cleaning of light fittings

Always check that a light is switched off, before cleaning.

1 Bulbs should be dusted and wiped over with a damp cloth regularly. Very dirty bulbs should be removed and washed in warm water and detergent, or wiped with methylated spirits. (Do not wet the metal cap.)
2 All light fittings should be dusted frequently.
3 Removable glass and plastic light fittings can be washed with warm water and detergent. They should be rinsed and wiped dry.
4 Parchment shades should be wiped with warm water and vinegar, and left to dry.
5 Fabric shades should be brushed frequently, or vacuumed with a suction attachment. Washable fabric shades can be washed in warm water and detergent, rinsed well and hung up to dry.
6 Stainless steel and chromium light fittings can be cleaned with warm water and detergent, and rubbed with a soft duster when dry.
7 Paper shades should be brushed frequently with a soft brush or feather duster.

Think and Do

1. What points would you look for when choosing:
a. a bed;
b. light fittings;
c. lounge furniture;
d. cutlery?

2. Copy this diagram into your notebook, under the heading, "Artificial lighting in the home".
3. Say how you would clean:
a. a polished dining table;
b. a dirty aluminium saucepan;
c. a glass light fitting;
d. a copper ornament;
e. an upholstered fireside chair;
f. a painted radiator.
4. Design a suitable light fitting for each of the following:
a. a sewing alcove;
b. a living room furnished with traditional furniture;
c. a small kitchen with poor natural lighting;
d. a child's bedroom.
5. Look through magazines and find pictures of furniture and fittings that you think are ***a.*** well-designed, ***b.*** badly designed. Stick them into your notebook under the two headings, and give reasons for your choice.
6. Find out the current price of:
a. a 60 watt bulb;
b. a wooden rolling pin;
c. a double bed with headboard;
d. a wooden standard lamp;
e. a linen basket;
f. a kitchen step-stool.
7. Clean a window using a modern window cleanser and then clean an adjacent window using warm water and a "leather". Say which you preferred to use and comment on the finished results.
8. Copy this diagram into your notebook and write a suitable sentence in each of the boxes.
9. List the advantages and disadvantages of:
a. buying second-hand furniture;
b. buying furniture on a hire purchase agreement;
c. making do-it-yourself furniture.
10. Visit your school and local libraries and find out all you can on different styles of traditional furniture. Prepare a classroom display.

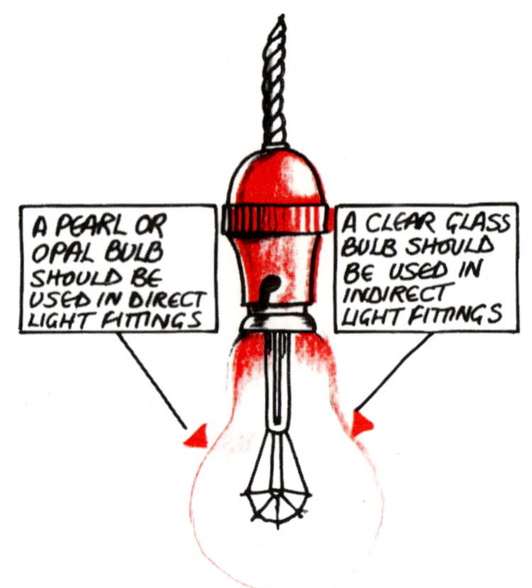

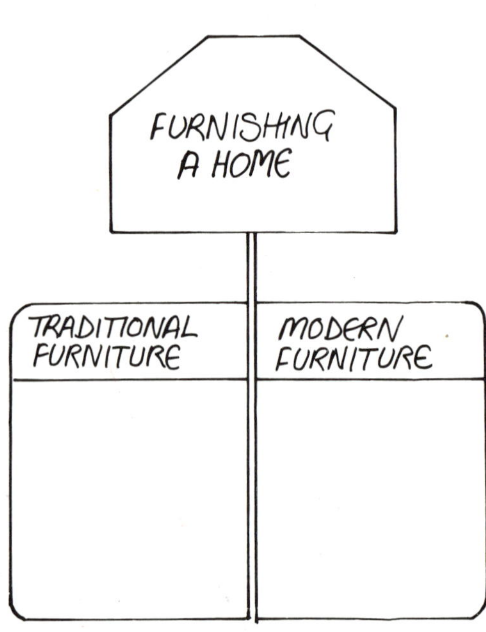

Part Three

Caring for a Home

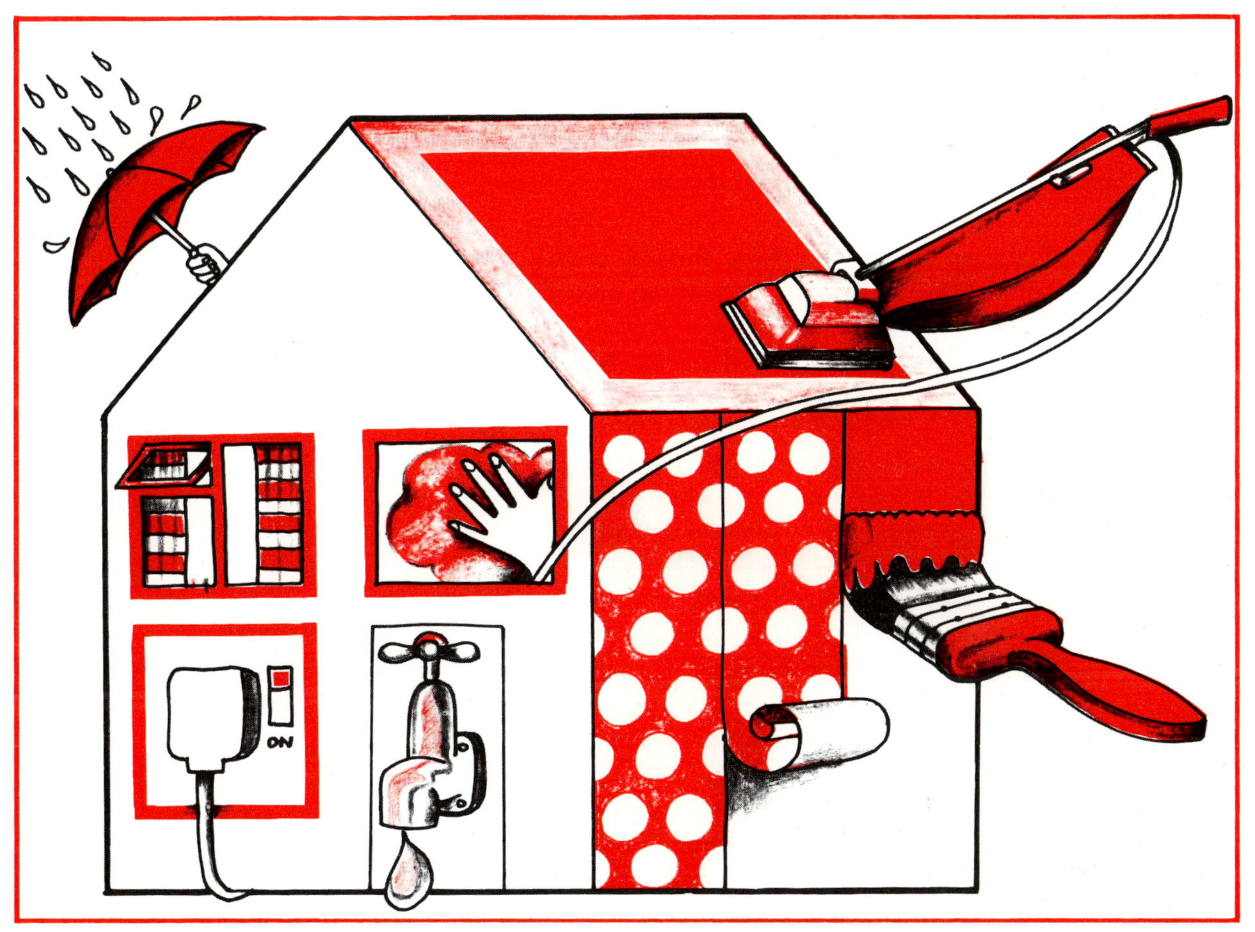

Organizing the housework

A housewife should be organized. She should know which jobs she intends to tackle during the day, and she should go about them in a methodical way without wasting time.

If a housewife plans her day sensibly, she will allow herself time for relaxation and for pursuing favourite hobbies. When the housework is done regularly, the odd day out shopping or the unexpected arrival of a friend, can be coped with easily, and the smooth running of the house is not affected. Below you will see an example of a day in the life of Mrs Brown, who has two young schoolchildren. Notice the length of the working day and how Mrs Brown has allowed herself free-time to use as she pleases.

7·30/8·45	Prepare breakfast. Get family ready for school/work. Take children to school.
8·50/9·15	Wash the breakfast dishes. Make the beds.
9·15/10·30	Do the daily cleaning of all rooms.
10·30/10·45	Coffee break (read the newspaper).
10·45/11·30	Do a weekly cleaning task.
11·30/12·00	Prepare lunch for family.
12·00/1·00	Have lunch. Clear away. See children back to school.
1·00/2·15	Do some baking. Wash up.
2·15/3·15	Free-time (spent in the garden or doing dressmaking).

3·15/4·00	Plan meals for the following day. Do the shopping. Meet the children from school.
4·05/4·30	Unpack shopping. See to the needs of the children.
4·30/5·00	Prepare evening meal.
5·0/6·15	Have evening meal. Clear the table. Wash the dishes. Watch the news on television.
6·15/7·30	See to the children. Games. Bath. Bed-time story.
7·30/9·45	Free-time (reading, knitting, watching television, attending evening classes, etc.)
9·45/10·15	Prepare light snack. Clear away. Lay the table for breakfast.
10·15	Go to bed.

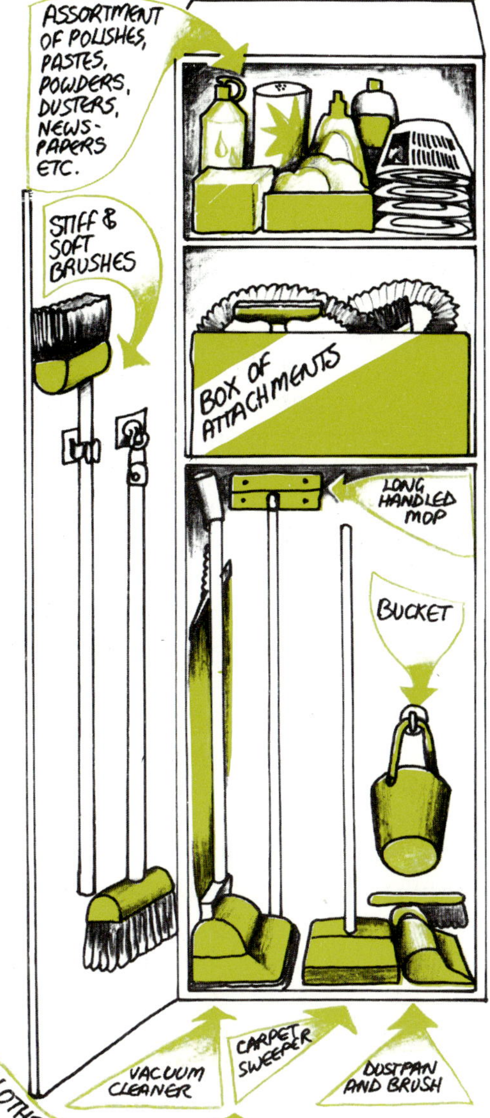

Cleaning equipment

It is a good idea to keep all cleaning equipment together. A broom cupboard with a top shelf is useful, because this provides space for storing bulky items such as long-handled brushes and vacuum cleaners, and also space on the shelf above for polishes, dusters and old newspapers. It should also contain:

CLEANSERS

- A PACKET OF WASHING SODA (for drains)
- A CLEANSING PASTE
- A SCOURING POWDER
- A TIN OF METAL POLISH
- A LAVATORY CLEANER
- A WAX FURNITURE POLISH OR -
- A SELF SHINE LIQUID OR SPRAY POLISH
- A WINDOW CLEANSER
- A NON SLIP FLOOR POLISH
- DETERGENT, WASHING POWDER, FABRIC CONDITIONER, STARCH, BLEACH } FOR THE FAMILY WASH
- CANISTER OF WASHING-UP LIQUID

CLEANING TOOLS

- A LONG HANDLED BRUSH WITH SOFT BRISTLES
- A LONG HANDLED BRUSH WITH STIFF BRISTLES
- A DUSTPAN AND BRUSH
- A LONG HANDLED MOP, A CARPET SWEEPER } OPTIONAL
- A VACUUM CLEANER & ATTACHMENTS
- A BUCKET
- A LAVATORY BRUSH

CLEANING CLOTHS

- DUSTERS
- POLISHING RAGS
- A FLOOR CLOTH
- A SPECIAL WINDOW CLOTH
- SCOURING PADS

A word about vacuum cleaners

There are many types of vacuum cleaner available. There are cylindrical, globular and upright models.

It is wise to buy a model that is convenient to use. It should be easy to lift and carry. Choose a model that has a good range of cleaning attachments. These are valuable aids in a busy household. (Even Dad may wish to borrow them when cleaning the car.) If you have a lot of stairs a cylindrical or globular model may be best.

Remember to empty vacuum cleaners regularly, and do check that flexes and plugs are ***safe*** to use.

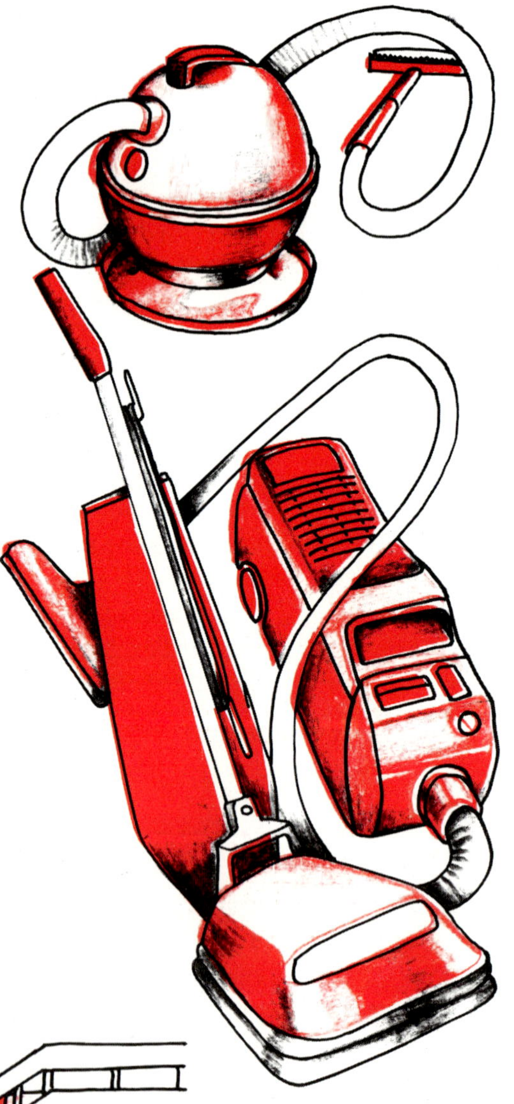

Daily cleaning

Daily cleaning is the term used to describe the day-to-day jobs that a housewife must do to keep her home ***tidy***, ***clean*** and ***well-organized***. A room that is allowed to become ***untidy*** will soon become ***dirty***. Each member of the family should be encouraged to tidy up his/her belongings. Even very young children can be persuaded to put away their toys, books and games, if they are allotted a special storage place.

When doing the daily cleaning in any room, a housewife should remember to:

a do the "dirty" tasks first (e.g. clean out the fire);
b see to the large surfaces in the room next;
c finish by dusting the small items.

Here are the daily cleaning jobs that should be done in each room.

Hall/Landing/Stairs

Bedrooms

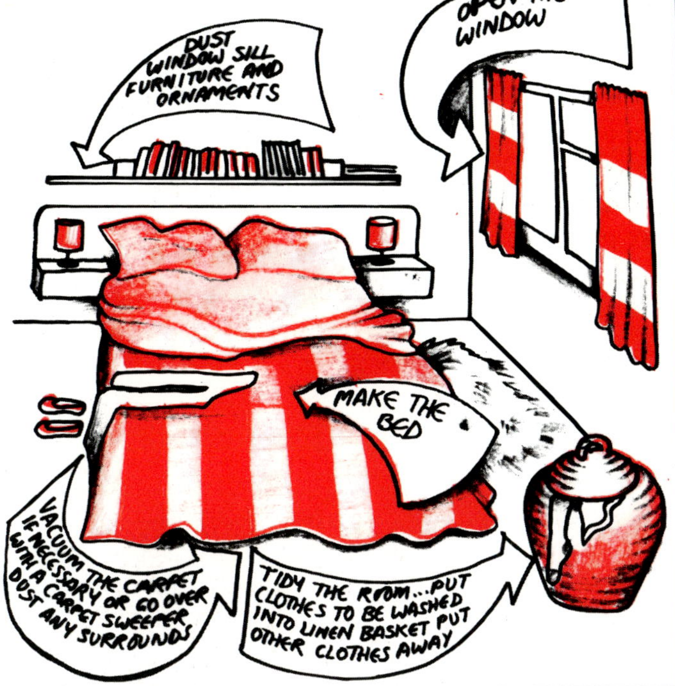
DUST WINDOW SILL FURNITURE AND ORNAMENTS
OPEN THE WINDOW
MAKE THE BED
VACUUM THE CARPET IF NECESSARY OR GO OVER WITH A CARPET SWEEPER DUST ANY SURROUNDS
TIDY THE ROOM...PUT CLOTHES TO BE WASHED INTO LINEN BASKET PUT OTHER CLOTHES AWAY

Bathroom/Lavatory

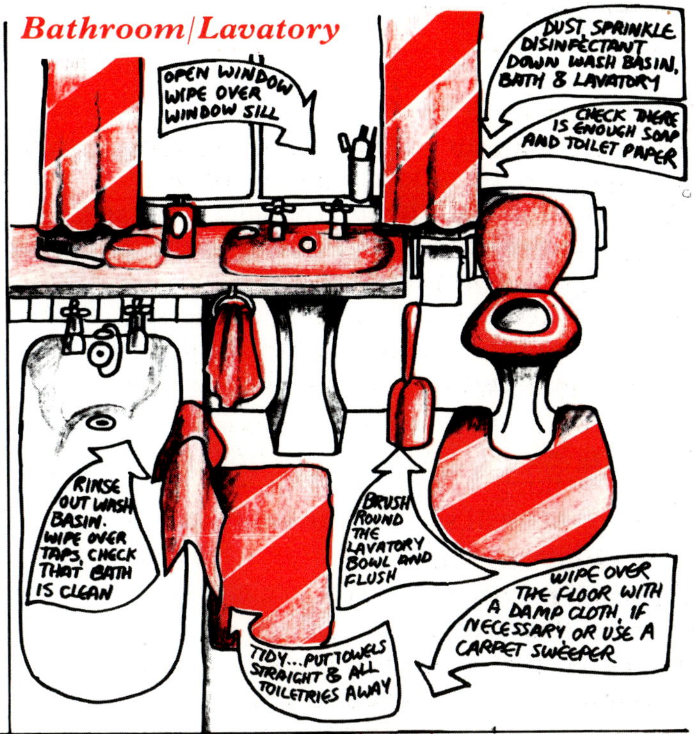
OPEN WINDOW WIPE OVER WINDOW SILL
DUST SPRINKLE DISINFECTANT DOWN WASH BASIN, BATH & LAVATORY
CHECK THERE IS ENOUGH SOAP AND TOILET PAPER
RINSE OUT WASH BASIN. WIPE OVER TAPS, CHECK THAT BATH IS CLEAN
BRUSH ROUND THE LAVATORY BOWL AND FLUSH
WIPE OVER THE FLOOR WITH A DAMP CLOTH, IF NECESSARY OR USE A CARPET SWEEPER
TIDY...PUT TOWELS STRAIGHT & ALL TOILETRIES AWAY

Living/Dining room

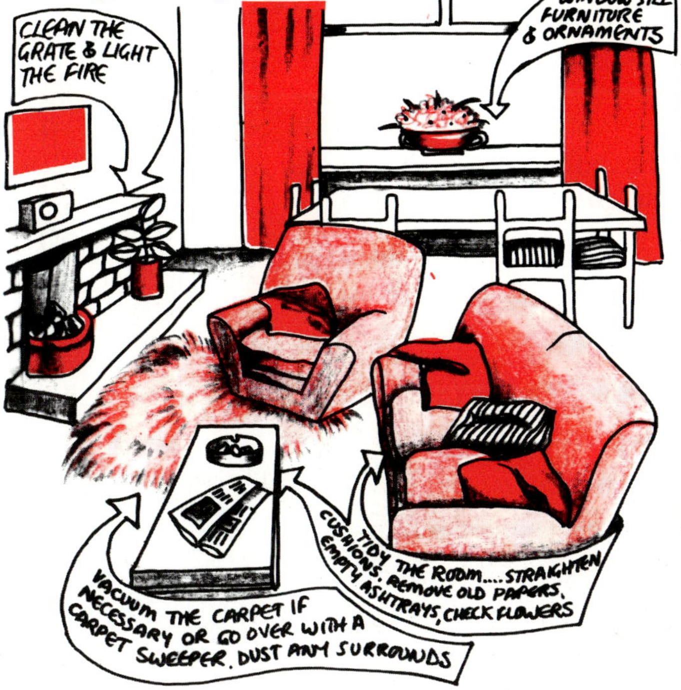
CLEAN THE GRATE & LIGHT THE FIRE
DUST WINDOW SILL FURNITURE & ORNAMENTS
TIDY THE ROOM.... STRAIGHTEN CUSHIONS, REMOVE OLD PAPERS, EMPTY ASHTRAYS, CHECK FLOWERS
VACUUM THE CARPET IF NECESSARY OR GO OVER WITH A CARPET SWEEPER. DUST ANY SURROUNDS

Kitchen

PUT ALL FOOD AWAY
MARCH
WASH-UP
WIPE OVER ALL WORKING SURFACES, WIPE OVER WINDOW SILL
TIDY-UP
EMPTY KITCHEN WASTE BIN
MOP THE FLOOR IF NECESSARY

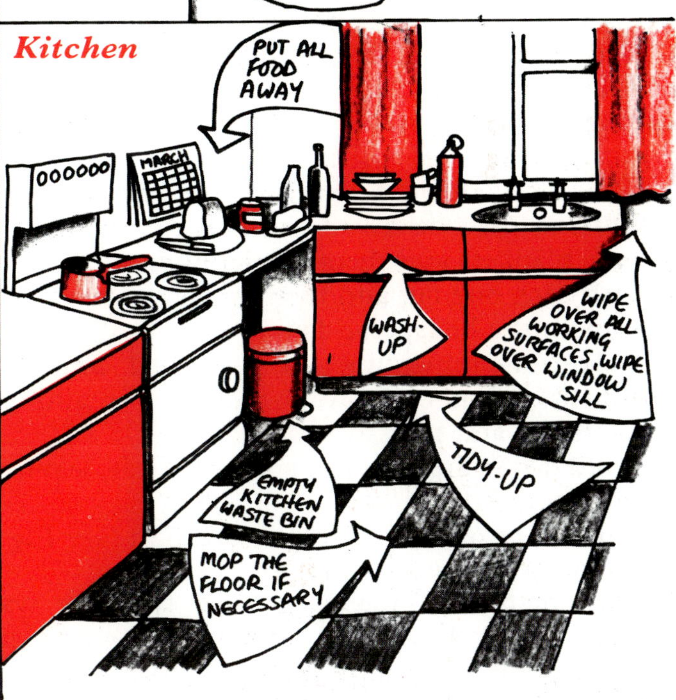

Cleaning out a fire

Put a sheet of newspaper over the carpet in front of the grate. Brush the soot from the back of the chimney and brush ash through the fire bars, leaving larger cinders only. Empty out ashpan into a bin or metal pail (in case ash is still slightly warm). Lay screwed-up newspaper in grate, cover with sticks or put in a firelighter. Add small coal. Brush or wipe down the hearth. Light the fire. Put a guard in front of it and remove the sheet of newspaper.

Making a bed

When making a bed, experiment and try to work out a method that will suit the position of your bed, and save you time and energy.

Here is a simple way to make a bed.

1 Stand along one side of the bed. Spread out the bottom sheet and tuck it in down the side.
2 Cover with the top sheet. Smooth flat and tuck in along the side.
3 Place the blankets on top. Tuck in.
4 Fold back the blankets and top sheet (about 50cm) leaving enough room for the pillow (see Fig. 1).
5 Put the pillow in position.
6 Cover one side of the bed with the bedspread.
7 Walk to the bottom of the bed. Throw back the bedspread, blankets and sheets. Starting with the bottom sheet smooth each one flat and tuck under the mattress.
8 Smooth the bedspread flat.
9 Walk to the remaining side of the bed. Smooth down the bottom sheet and tuck under. Pull the remaining sheet and blankets flat and tuck in.
10 Fold down the blankets and top sheet, leaving room for the pillow.
11 Put the remaining pillow in position (see Fig. 2).
12 Cover with the bedspread.

This method of making a bed cuts the walking and bending involved to a minimum. Always try to get neat corners at the bottom of the bed. Fully- and semi-fitted sheets do help. Bedmaking can be made easier by using a continental-style quilt (see page 91).

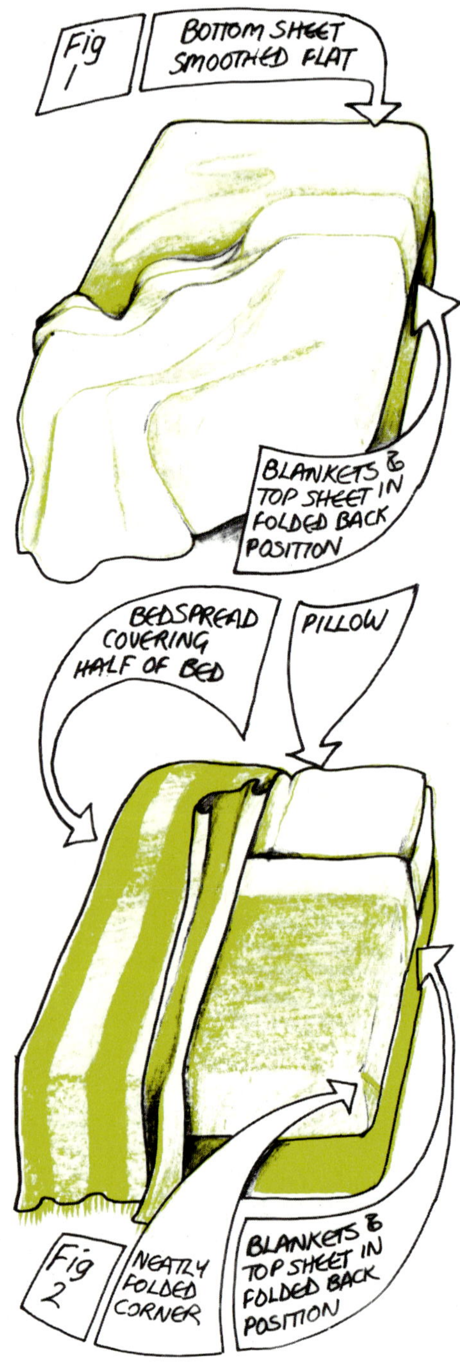

Weekly cleaning

You will have noticed that daily cleaning consisted mainly of keeping a home looking tidy. Weekly cleaning, however, refers to the cleaning of the furniture and fittings in each room. It is necessary each week to:

- *a* wash the floors in the kitchen, bathroom and lavatory;
- *b* take outside all loose mats and give them a good shake.

In addition to these tasks, a housewife should try to fit in any of the following jobs when they need doing:

1 Clean windows and mirrors.
2 Polish wooden furniture.
3 Clean upholstered furniture, using the attachments from a vacuum cleaner or a stiff, upholstery brush.
4 Clean and polish metal ornaments, fittings, handles, etc.
5 Vacuum and clean under chairs, tables, settees and beds. Shaped attachments should be used to clean into the corners and ledges of rooms.
6 Dust lampshades, light fittings, high ledges, tops of pelmets and pictures. A feather duster can be useful.
7 Wash down tiles in the kitchen, bathroom and lavatory.

Obviously, all these cleaning tasks cannot be done in one day, and a sensible housewife will space out her weekly cleaning. (Remember Mrs Brown?) A housewife may choose to do the weekly cleaning in the living room on one day, and then tackle another room on the next day. She may choose one day to concentrate on a particular type of surface, e.g. windows or painted wooden surfaces.

When doing the weekly cleaning in any room, a housewife should work in a methodical way. She should begin by doing any "dirty" jobs. Then she should tackle high areas in a room, gradually working her way downwards. The large surfaces of a room should be cleaned next followed by the small surfaces. Dusting should be done last of all.

A working housewife will not be able to tackle many of these weekly cleaning tasks, but she should see that the kitchen, living room, bathroom and lavatory are cleaned regularly. The remaining jobs will have to be fitted in when time and energy allows.

Special cleaning

If a housewife has been conscientious about the regular cleaning of a home, there will be little special cleaning to be done. There are, however, some special jobs.

1 Blankets, cushion covers and curtains should be cleaned periodically.
2 Chimneys must be swept twice a year.
3 Cupboards, drawers and wardrobes should be cleaned out.
4 Carpets may need shampooing.

Organizing the housework when working full-time

Many housewives have a full-time job outside the home. They often do this to increase the family income, to make new friends or because they need an added interest.

A housewife who has a full-time job must fit in her housework when she can. Some tasks will have to be done each morning before she goes to work.

1 Beds will have to be made.
2 The breakfast dishes must be washed up.
3 Coal fires must be cleaned out and laid ready for the evening.
4 Vegetables may need to be prepared for the evening meal.
5 The living room should be tidied.
6 Young children must be got ready for school.

It is a good idea for a working housewife to get the other members of her family to help in this morning ritual. Children should be encouraged to make their own beds and clean their own shoes before going to school, and they can even help to clear up after breakfast. A helpful husband will also play his part, by doing one or two jobs around the house before going out to work. He may offer to do some shopping on his way home at night. This organization of the housework should be a family affair. If each member knows what he or she is expected to do each morning, the jobs will be done more efficiently. If there does not seem to be enough time to do all these tasks before leaving for work, then a housewife should ***get up half an hour earlier.***

There is nothing more depressing than to return to a cold, cheerless house after a full day's work, to find this ►
Do not let this happen in your home.

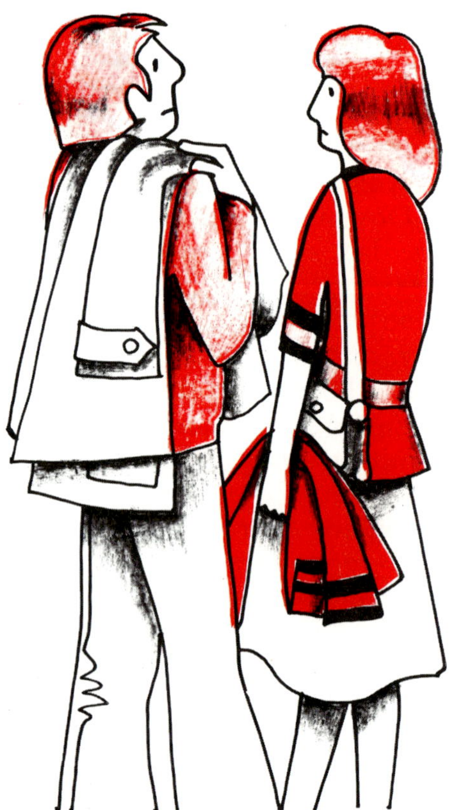

The evening chores should also be shared. If each member of a family is allotted one particular task, a housewife's job will be made much easier. After the evening meal, a working housewife will need to relax. She must give herself some time to "unwind" from the tensions of the day. She may wish to read a book; do the crossword in the newspaper; watch television or pursue a favourite hobby. Later in the evening, she may wish to fit in a simple household task, e.g. ironing or mending clothes, but most of the chores will have to be left until the weekend. A well-organized working housewife will probably choose to do a lot of the household cleaning jobs on a Friday evening, knowing that she has not got to go to work the following morning and can have an extra hour in bed.

Remember that a working housewife should:

- ***a*** always make time for relaxation;
- ***b*** fit in her housework when she can;
- ***c*** expect other members of her family to help.

She may wish to:

- ***a*** invest in an automatic washing machine, or use a laundry or launderette for the family wash;
- ***b*** invest in as much labour-saving equipment as she can afford;
- ***c*** employ "help" to do some jobs in the house;
- ***d*** use "convenience" and ready-frozen foods for week-day meals.

Think and Do

1. What advice would you give to a working housewife on:
a. doing the family wash;
b. shopping for food?
2. Make a list of the cleaning agents you would expect to find in a modern kitchen.
3. Collect as many pictures as you can, of different types of vacuum cleaner. Stick them into your notebook. Choose which model you like best and give reasons for your choice.

4. Say how you would:
a. clean a carpeted staircase;
b. clear a grate and light a coal fire;
c. remove fingermarks from a mirror;
d. do the daily cleaning in a lavatory.
5. Find out the current prices of:
a. a long-handled stiff brush;
b. a tin of scouring powder;
c. a duster;
d. a large tin of black shoe polish;
e. a lavatory brush and holder;
f. a tin of self-shine spray polish for furniture;
g. a carpet sweeper;
h. a window "leather".
6. Look at the picture of a living room. List the daily cleaning jobs that need to be done and give the correct order for them.
7. Find out all you can on the household cleaning methods used by your grandmother. Make a list of the cleaning agents she used and draw pictures of the equipment she had to help her.
8. Suggest an evening meal that a working housewife might prepare for her family.
9. Name a suitable cleaning agent for each of the following:
a. a bath;
b. a window sill;
c. a mahogany coffee table;
d. a formica-topped kitchen table;
e. a brass ornament;
f. a plastic lampshade.
10. Copy the following diagram into your notebook and write suitable sentences in each of the boxes.

Simple home decorating

Many people feel that decorating a room is too difficult a job for them to tackle. It certainly can be hard work but it can also be very rewarding. There is much pleasure to be gained from "doing-it-yourself", and with a little experience and plenty of patience there is no reason that the result should not be pleasing.

Preparing a room

It is important to prepare a room before starting to decorate.

1 As much furniture as possible should be removed. Any furniture that cannot be put into another room should be moved to the middle of the room and covered with old sheets.

2 Curtains should be taken down. This is a good time to launder them or have them dry cleaned.

3 Ornaments, pictures, mirrors, pelmets and lamp fittings should be removed to a safe place.

4 Carpets should either be rolled up and taken into another room, or be covered with old sheets, polythene or newspaper.

5 The room should be dusted thoroughly and the floor swept clean.

6 All the surfaces in the room should be washed down. Use warm water and a detergent, or special decorator's sugar soap that can be bought at a do-it-yourself shop. Rinse well. Do not overwet the ceiling.

7 Any cracks in the plaster on the walls or ceiling should be filled with a cellulose filler and then rubbed smooth with glass paper after the filling has dried. Cracks in woodwork can be filled in a similar way.

8 Paintwork should be smoothed down using "wet and dry" glass paper. For a really professional finish, always remove door handles before decorating.

9 Old wallpaper should be scraped from the walls. A special wallpaper stripping solution can be used which will thoroughly wet the wallpaper, making it easier to remove. Vinyl wallpapers need to be scored so that the wetting solution can penetrate and soften the wallpaper.

10 All cleaning equipment should be put away before the materials for decorating the room are brought out.

A reminder about colour schemes

Do remember that colour schemes can have a dramatic effect on a room.

Types of paint

There are two main types of paint available and it is important to know for which surfaces each one is suitable.

1 ***Gloss paint.*** This is suitable for the top coating on external and internal woodwork. It has a hard, shiny surface when dry, and is washable. Some gloss paints have polyurethane, silthane or other additives to improve their toughness.

2 ***Emulsion paint.*** This is easy to use and dries quickly to give a matt finish. It is suitable for plastered internal surfaces, such as ceilings and walls, but it can also be used externally. Emulsion paint can be sponged clean. A vinyl emulsion paint gives a tougher finish which can be scrubbed clean. It is therefore suitable for areas that dirty easily.

Eggshell paint is a top-coat finish that dries to a dull shine. It is suitable for internal surfaces. Gloss, eggshell and emulsion paints can be bought in gel-form. These are ***thixotropic*** paints and will spread easily without dripping.

Paint can be applied with:

- a brush;
- a roller and tray;
- a pad and tray.

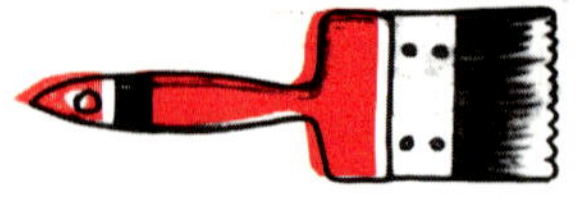

Points to remember when painting

1 If a skin has formed on top of the paint, this should be removed carefully before the paint is stirred. (The non-drip paints should not be stirred.)

2 Use paint sparingly. Do not overwet brushes, rollers or paint pads. Remember that several thin coats of paint give a better finish than one thick coat.

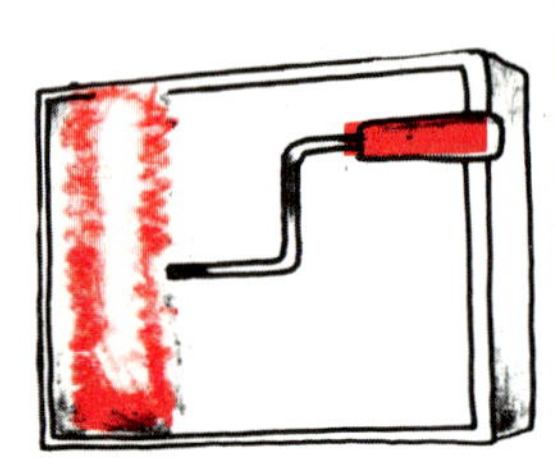

3 Let each coat of paint dry before applying another coat. Wooden surfaces usually require two coats: an undercoat and a top-coat. Plastered surfaces require two coats of emulsion paint.
4 Paint brushes, rollers and pads should be cleaned immediately after use. If an oil-based paint has been used (gloss, undercoat, thixotropic), the brush should be cleaned in a turpentine substitute, and then washed in warm, soapy water. If an emulsion paint has been used, a rinse in warm water is sufficient. Always let brushes, rollers and pads dry thoroughly before putting them away.

A rag that has been dampened with turpentine substitute will come in handy for wiping up spills. ***Be prepared.*** Some gloss paints contain lead. This type of paint should ***never*** be used indoors. Lead is very poisonous and there is always the danger that young children will suck or bite wooden surfaces that have been treated with lead paint, and in this way swallow the poison. Always check that gloss paint for use inside a house is lead-free and thus avoid danger.

Types of wallpaper

There are four main types of wallpaper available and it is important to know for which room each one is suitable.
1 ***Ordinary wallpaper.*** This can vary in quality and thickness, but it cannot be washed clean. It would therefore be unsuitable for kitchens and bathrooms, and areas such as children's bedrooms that may quickly get marked. It is more suitable for living areas and adult bedrooms. This type of wallpaper can be bought in a wide range of colours and patterns, with a rough or smooth surface.
2 ***Washable wallpaper.*** This type of wallpaper can be wiped over with a damp cloth but it cannot be scrubbed clean. It is suitable for kitchens and bathrooms.
3 ***Vinyl-coated wallpaper.*** This type of wallpaper is very tough and can be scrubbed clean. It is, therefore, very suitable for "dirty" areas in a home, e.g. kitchens, bathrooms, children's rooms and staircase walls. A vinyl-coated wallpaper can be bought in a wide range of colours and patterns, and can be used in any area in a home.

4 Ready-pasted wallpaper. This type of wallpaper is a good quality grade of wallpaper, usually with a vinyl coating, and can be used in any area in a home. The paste is already on the paper and it functions once the paper has been dampened.

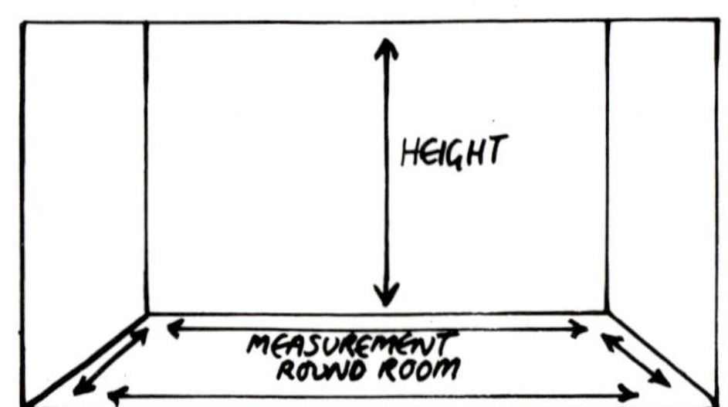

A good quality paper usually requires a lining paper underneath. Check with the shop assistant if you are in doubt about this.

Wallpaper can be hung from the walls with a cold water paste or a cellulose paste. When mixing packet pastes always follow the instructions on the packet. Check that you buy the right kind of paste for the wallpaper you are using. Vinyl wallpapers require a special adhesive.

Points to remember when wallpapering

1 To calculate how many rolls of wallpaper you will need, measure the room carefully. You will need to know the height of the room (from skirting board to ceiling), and the measurement all round the walls. Take these measurements along to the shop with you. You will be able to consult a chart in the shop which will tell you how many rolls you will need to buy, for the room measurements you have calculated.

2 Make sure that each roll of wallpaper has the same colour code. Colours may vary slightly in different batches of wallpaper, so do check this.

3 If you are going to use a lining paper, this goes on the wall first. Hang the lining paper in horizontal strips, before hanging the wallpaper in vertical strips.

4 Cut a strip of wallpaper the length of the wall plus 8cm. This will allow for wastage at the top and bottom of the strip, when neatening the edges.

5 Each succeeding strip should be cut with the pattern matching.

6 Spread the paste on the wrong side of the wallpaper, working on a flat surface. You can use a kitchen table or proper pasting table for this. Fold the wallpaper carefully and leave it to soften. Five minutes is sufficient for ordinary wallpapers and ten minutes for heavy ones.

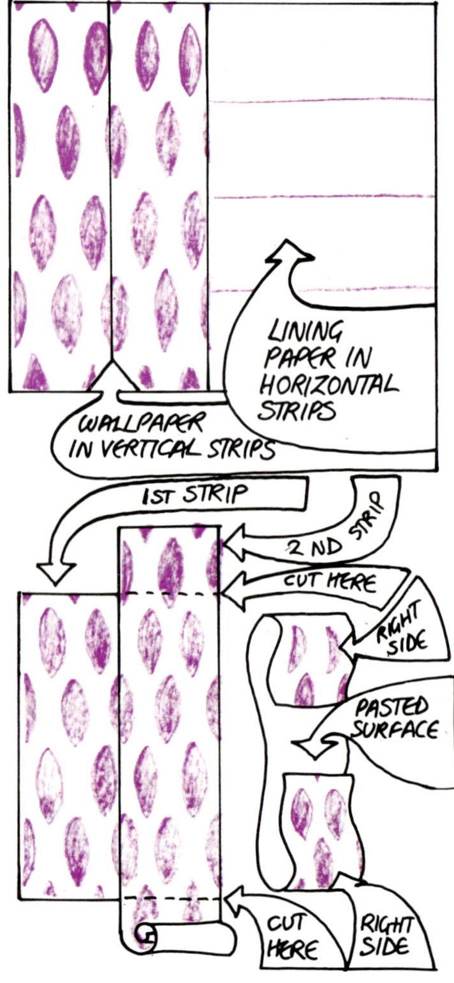

7 Draw a straight line down the wall using a weight on a piece of string as a guideline. Hold the first strip of wallpaper by the top two corners and slide it into position. Smooth away any air bubbles with a dry sponge, as the wallpaper unfolds.
8 Using the back edge of a knife, mark the crease where the top of the wallpaper should be trimmed. Carefully peel the wallpaper back and cut along the crease mark. Trim the bottom edge in a similar way.
9 Work round the room, working away from the window, matching each length of paper. Do not overlap the edges.
10 Care must be taken when fitting wallpaper around light switches, window and door frames.
11 Any paste which has squeezed on to the wallpaper, ceiling or skirting board should be wiped off immediately with a clean, damp cloth.
12 Ready-pasted wallpapers should be soaked in water before being used. A special trough can be bought for this purpose or you can use the bath.

Think and Do

1. List the preparations you would make in a living room before starting to re-decorate.
2. Draw and colour a design for a nursery wallpaper.
3. How would you:
a. clean a paint brush after using vinyl emulsion paint;
b. prepare the surface of a door that is to be painted;
c. protect a fitted carpet when decorating?
4. Suggest a colour scheme for each of the following rooms:
a. a small, cold kitchen;
b. a large, airy living room;
c. a dark hall and staircase.
5. Are these sentences ***true*** or ***false***?
a. A gloss paint is suitable for external and internal woodwork.
b. Sugar soap can be used for washing down paintwork.

c. A thixotropic paint is a thin paint that drips easily from a brush.
d. A turpentine substitute should be used for cleaning emulsion paint from brushes and rollers.
e. A vinyl-coated wallpaper cannot be washed.
f. A high ceiling can be made to look lower by using a dark colour.

6. Write a poem entitled "Colours".

7. Find out the current prices for each of the following:
a. turpentine substitute;
b. a paint roller and tray;
c. a packet of wallpaper stripper;
d. a packet of cellulose filler;
e. a litre of good quality brilliant white gloss paint;
f. a litre of good quality coloured vinyl emulsion paint;
g. a sheet of "wet and dry" glass paper;
h. a small packet of adhesive paste for vinyl wallpaper.

8. Cut squares of different wallpapers. An old sample book would be useful. Make your own folder of wallpaper designs.

9. Copy out this crossword and complete it.

Clues across
1. Used when wallpapering.
2. This type of wallpaper is washable.
3. Can be used when painting.

Clues down
4. Should be removed from a tin of paint.
5. Paint is bought by this measurement.
6. A top-coat paint.

10. List the advantages and disadvantages of decorating a room yourself, rather than paying a decorator to do it for you.

Simple home maintenance

In this chapter we shall learn how to do simple maintenance jobs about the home.

Understanding our water supply

We all take for granted the water supply that is piped to our homes. Try to imagine what would happen if all the taps suddenly ran dry. How would we cope? Water is essential to life.

Water is brought to cities, towns and villages along thick underground pipes. These pipes are called mains. A service pipe takes water from the mains directly to each house or block of flats. This supply of water can be controlled by a stop tap (stop valve) which is situated outside the building, often underneath the pavement. A small metal cover will show you where the stop tap on your service pipe is located. There is another stop tap where the service pipe has entered the house. Have a look at home and see if you can find these two stop taps. Stop taps are turned ***clockwise*** to close and ***anti-clockwise*** to open.

How to clear a blocked sink

Sinks can become blocked by tea leaves, grease and particles of food that collect in the U bend trap (see page 36). If water remains in the sink after the plug has been removed, this indicates a blocked pipe. To remove the blockage you will need to use a force pump. Place the force pump over the plug-hole, press down firmly and then pull the force pump up sharply. Repeat this movement several times to clear the blockage. After the water in the sink has drained away, run fresh hot water down the drain.

If the blockage remains after using a force pump, then the U bend trap will have to be emptied by unscrewing the nut. ***Before*** doing this, place a bucket underneath the trap.

1 Carefully unscrew the nut, allowing the water in the trap to drain into the bucket.

2 Using a coiled piece of wire, clean each side of the trap with a twisting movement.
3 Run a little hot water down the sink. Remember to keep the bucket in position.
4 If the pipe is clear, then replace the nut.
5 Run fresh hot water down the drain to rinse the pipes and to refill the U bend trap.

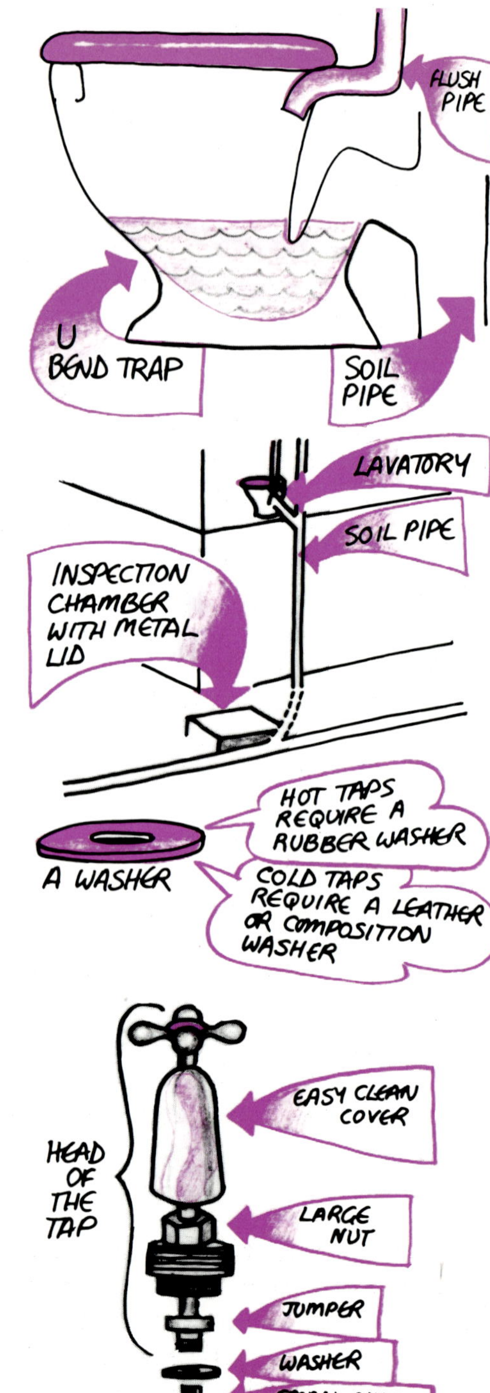

How to clear a blocked lavatory

A lavatory has a U bend trap which may occasionally become blocked. Sanitary towels, soluble nappies and newspaper are the main offenders.

If a lavatory will not empty after being flushed, then repeat the flushing process. Often the force of the water will remove the blockage and flush it down the soil pipe. If this does not happen, then a stiff lavatory brush can be used to clear the blockage. Remember to thoroughly clean and disinfect the brush after use.

Sometimes the blockage is where the soil pipe empties into the drain. Look for the metal lid that covers the inspection chamber. This will be outside but near to the soil pipe. Lift the cover. If the cause of the blockage is apparent it can often be removed by special rods. These rods can be borrowed from the sanitary department of your local authority.

Occasionally the blockage is in the soil pipe itself and cannot be easily reached. If this happens, pour disinfectant down the lavatory and contact a plumber.

How to change the washer on a tap

If a tap drips continually or makes a humming and thumping noise when you turn it, you will need to fit a new washer. These can be bought from a do-it-yourself or ironmonger's shop. When you have bought the right kind of washer, you will need to collect an adjustable spanner. Always turn ***off*** the stop tap and turn ***on*** the tap before you begin. This will empty the water from the pipe.

1 Unscrew the easy-clean cover and carefully unscrew the large nut using the adjustable spanner.
2 Lift up the head of the tap and the jumper.

3 Unscrew the small nut that is holding the washer in position.
4 Remove the old washer and fit a new one.
5 Tighten the small nut.
6 Replace the jumper and the head of the tap.
7 Tighten the large nut with the spanner.
8 Screw down the easy-clean cover.
9 Turn the tap ***off*** and the stop tap ***on*** and check that the tap is working properly.

How to stop an overflow from a cistern

An overflow pipe passes from each cistern in a house, through the nearest wall to the outside. The cold water tank will have an overflow and so will each lavatory cistern. The overflow pipe is a safety device to prevent flooding. If an overflow drips it is a sign that too much water is building up inside the cistern, and that the floating ball and ball valve are not working correctly.

When a cistern fills with water, the ball rises closing the valve and cutting off the water (Fig. A). When the cistern empties, the ball falls with the level of water, and opens the valve allowing water to refill the cistern (Fig. B). If an overflow continues to drip, it is possible that the lever of the floating ball has become bent. Gently bend the arm of the lever downwards. If this does not stop the overflow from dripping, the cause could be:

- ***a*** a faulty washer that needs to be replaced;
- ***b*** a dirty ball valve that needs to be cleaned;
- ***c*** a leaking ball that needs to be replaced. (This is easily recognized because the ball will have sunk to the bottom of the cistern.)

In any of these cases it would be wise to call a plumber.

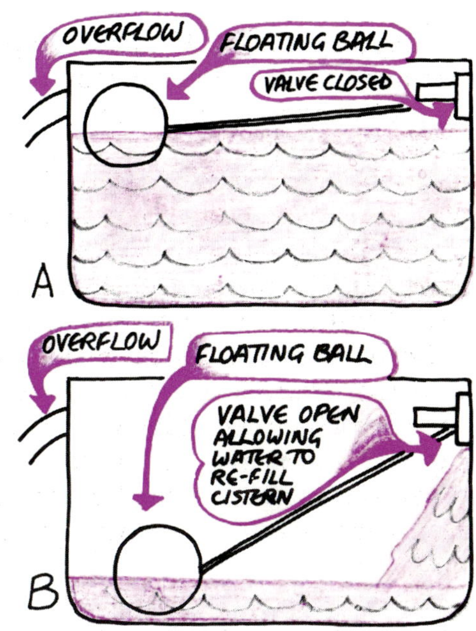

How to prevent water pipes from freezing and bursting

When liquids freeze, they expand (grow bigger). This expansion can cause water pipes to crack. When the ice thaws, water seeps through the crack in the pipe causing flooding. There are several precautions that you can take to prevent this happening.

1 All taps should be turned off securely. A dripping tap could cause the waste pipe to freeze up and then the sink would overflow. If a tap needs a new washer, attend to this job before the winter. Keep the plugs to all sinks and to the bath, tightly in position.

2 Any water pipes that are outside or near an external wall should be lagged. This can be done by wrapping rags, strips of sacking or specially-bought felt around the exposed pipes to protect them from cold winds and frost.

3 Try to keep the house as warm as possible by stopping draughts from ill-fitting windows and doors, and by keeping room doors closed.

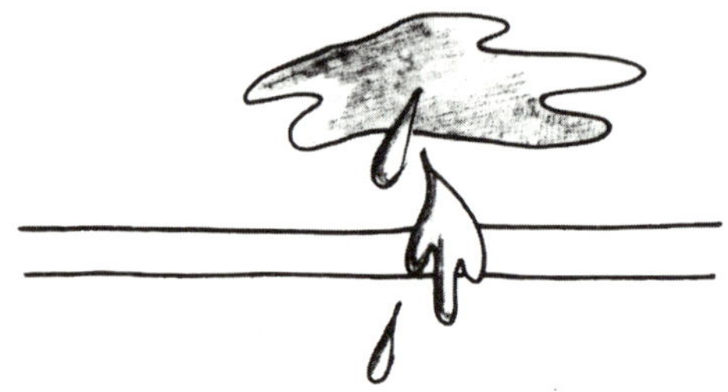

4 It is a good idea to sprinkle salt around the metal cover to the outside stop tap. Can you think why?

5 If you are leaving the house empty for more than a day during winter, turn off the stop tap and drain the water from the pipes by turning on all the taps and by flushing the lavatory. ***Do remember to turn on the water when you return before lighting any boiler fires.*** This is very important. If you have an automatically-controlled central heating system that is time-set to operate whilst you are away, ***do not do this***. If you have a solid fuel central heating system or if you are switching an automatically-controlled system ***off***, then it is a wise precaution to drain the water from the pipes during very cold spells.

What to do when water pipes freeze

If, in spite of your precautions, a water pipe does freeze, try to thaw the ice by covering the pipe with rags that have been soaked in hot water. A small portable heater placed near the pipe will also help. If it does not thaw out, send for a plumber.

What to do when water pipes burst

1 Keep calm.

2 Quickly turn ***off*** the water at the stop tap and turn ***on*** the taps to sinks and the bath. If you have a central heating system that pumps water through radiators, turn off the pump. Fires with a back boiler and solid fuel boilers for central heating systems should be emptied. This must be done quickly but carefully by scooping the embers into a metal bucket or dustbin lid, and carrying them outside.

3 Call a plumber.

4 Try to make a temporary repair to the burst pipe while you are waiting for the plumber. Rags can be used to plug and wrap around the burst pipe. Cover these with any waterproof tape or material that you have handy.

Understanding our electricity supply

It is during a power cut that we realize how much we have come to rely on electricity in our modern homes.

Electricity can be very dangerous if used carelessly. Never attempt any electrical repairs unless you know exactly what you are doing.

Electricity is produced at a power station and carried by pylons and wires to our cities, towns and villages. It is brought to our homes by underground cables, and enters each house or flat through a meter and fuse box that has a main switch. Have a look at home and see if you can find the electricity meter and fuse box. They may be in the hall, pantry, cellar, garage or living room.

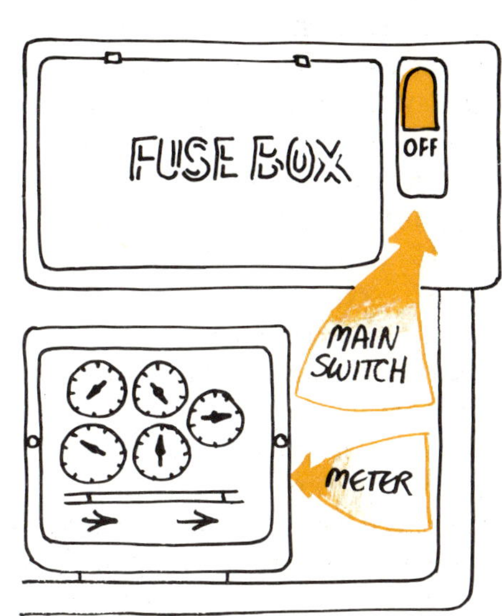

Before attempting any electrical repairs or inspections, always turn the main switch to the ***off*** position. This will cut off the electrical current.

How to read an electric meter

Electricity is bought by the ***unit***. The Electricity Board works out how many units of electricity have been used during each period of the year, and a bill is sent for the required amount. The amount of electricity used is calculated by reading the dials on the meter.

1 Concentrate on the four large dials.
2 Read the dials from left to right.
3 Write down the number that the finger has just passed, e.g. if the finger is pointing between the numbers 5 and 6, write down 5.

The meter in the diagram reads: dial 1 — 6; dial 2 — 5; dial 3 — 2; dial 4 — 9. Therefore 6529 units of electricity have been used. It is easy to work out the amount of electricity that has been used during any period, by subtracting the last known reading from the present reading.

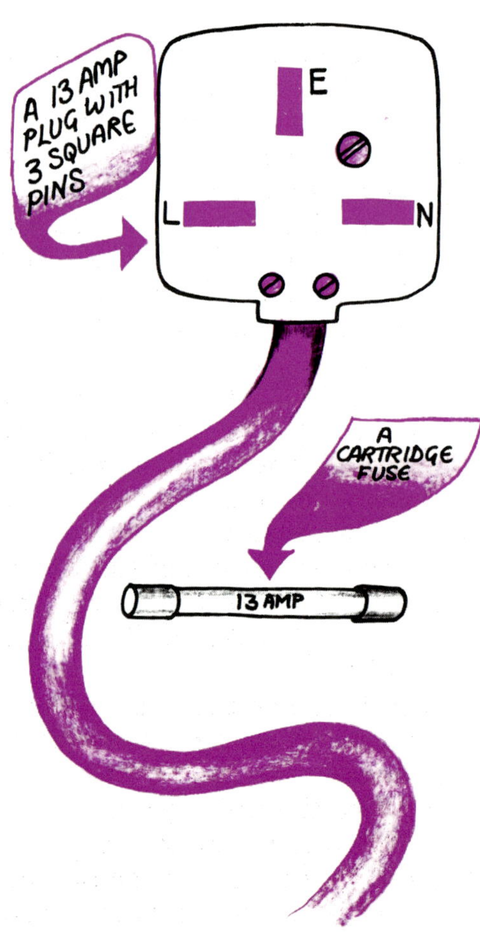

How to wire a plug

Modern houses are fitted with sockets that will take 13 amp plugs with square pins. Older-type houses may still have sockets for 5 or 15 amp plugs with round pins. When a 13 amp plug is unscrewed you will see that it has three terminals which are marked:

E (earth)
L (live)
N (neutral)

It also has a socket which will take a cartridge fuse.

A fuse is a safety device which prevents wiring from overheating and possibly causing a fire. If too great an electric current is passed along a wire, the fuse or weakest point will "blow" and break the circuit. Plugs should be fitted with either a 3 amp cartridge fuse (for appliances less than 750 watts), or a 13 amp cartridge fuse (for appliances of 750–3000 watts). The wattage for each household appliance should be clearly marked. Do check.

The flex from an electrical appliance contains three wires which are coloured green/yellow, brown, and blue.

1 Thread the flex under the cord grip and check that each wire is long enough to reach its terminal easily.

Green/Yellow	wire to the E (earth terminal)
Brown	wire to the L (live terminal)
Blue	wire to the N (neutral terminal)

2 Connect the wires to the terminals and screw down.
3 Check that the correct fuse is in position.
4 Screw the plug together.
5 Insulation tape should be bound round the flex where it enters the plug.

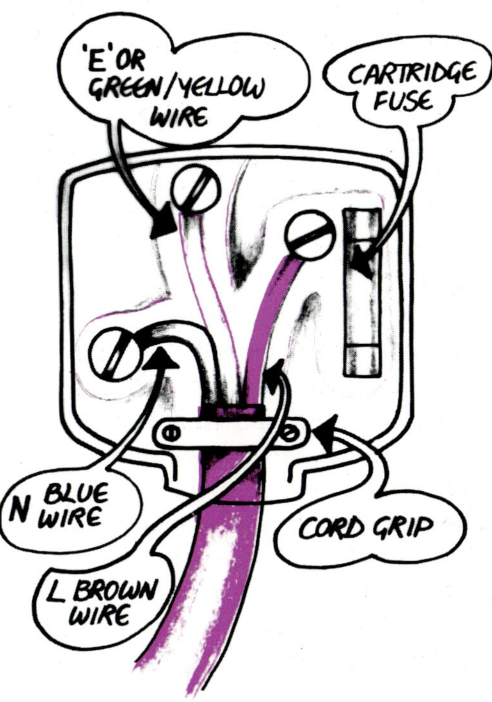

How to mend a fuse

If any household appliance will not work when plugged in, it is possible that the fuse has blown. ***Switch off*** and ***pull out the plug***. Unscrew the plug and see if the cartridge fuse looks black and charred. If it does, the fuse must be replaced (using the correct rating). Try to find out why the fuse has blown. It could be that the fuse was old and faulty, or it could be that the wires in the plug were touching. If this is so, the appliance will continue to fuse until the fault has been repaired.

If you need to rewire a fuse in the household fuse box, always ***switch off*** the main switch first. A card of fuse wire and a torch should be kept in a handy place so that you are not searching for these items in the dark.

1 Pull out the fuses one at a time and look for the one that has a broken wire.
2 Remove the pieces of fused wire but notice how each end has been attached. Cut a new length of wire from the card. Use the correct rating. This should be printed above each fuse holder.
3 Attach one end of the wire, screwing clockwise, and the other end, screwing anti-clockwise. Tighten the screws at each end.
4 Replace the fuse holder.
5 Turn on the main switch.

If the same fuse blows again, you should contact an electrician who will test the various appliances on the circuit.

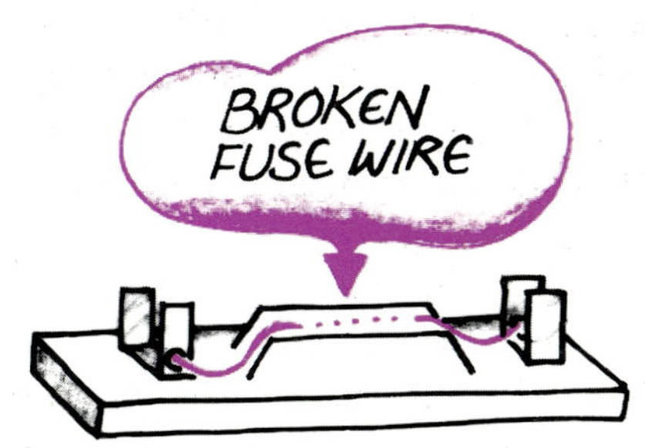

Understanding our gas supply

Gas is brought to homes along underground pipes. Modern gas appliances are well-designed and easy to use, but they should be serviced regularly. Care should be taken to see that all gas equipment is working efficiently. A small leak of gas can build up gradually with possible fatal results.

What to do when you smell leaking gas

1 Quickly check to see if any pilot lights have blown out, or if any gas tap has been turned on accidentally. If you cannot find an obvious cause for the gas leak, turn off the gas at the main and check that all gas taps are in the off position. Telephone the Gas Board immediately. If you discover that a pilot light or gas ring has blown out, do not apply a light. Turn off the tap and ventilate the room well. When the smell of gas has disappeared, re-light in the usual way.
2 ***Never*** look for a gas leak with a lighted match or candle.
3 If you do smell gas and cannot trace its source, put out all naked flames. Do not smoke.

How to read a gas meter

If you pay for your gas supply with a coin meter, then always be careful if the gas runs out. Turn off the gas taps and pilot lights before putting another coin in the meter. When the gas comes on, re-light all pilot lights.

Your gas meter will be read at intervals of the year, and a bill will be sent for the required amount, if you have not been paying by the slot meter method. To calculate how much gas has been used during any period, look at the dials on the meter.

Concentrate on the four main dials. Ignore the two that ·ve red pointers.

2 Read the dials from left to right.
3 Write down the number that the finger has just passed, e.g. if the finger is pointing between numbers 7 and 8, write down 7.
4 Add 00 after the last figure. The meter in the diagram reads: 529400. Therefore 529400 cu ft of gas have been used. Gas is paid for in ***therms***. To change cu ft into therms, you must know the heating power or calorific value (CV) of the gas in your area which will be shown on your gas bill. The simple calculation is to multiply the hundreds of cubic feet by the calorific value and divide by 1000. For example, if 9600 cu ft of gas have been used since the last reading was taken and the calorific value is 500, this is

$$\frac{96 \times 500}{1000} = 48 \text{ therms}$$

Once the metric system is fully in use, instead of therms the calculation will be in megajoules (1 therm = 105·5 megajoules).

Think and Do

1. Write a poem entitled "Power cut".
2. Copy the following sentences into your notebooks using the correct word which you will choose from those words in the brackets:

a. When a liquid freezes, it (***expands***, ***contracts***).
b. Electricity is bought by the (***unit***, ***therm***) and gas is bought by the (***unit***, ***therm***).
c. When reading a gas meter, you should always add (***00***, ***000***) after the last figure.
d. If you have a burst pipe, turn (***on***, ***off***) the stop tap and turn (***on***, ***off***) the taps.
e. Modern household electrical sockets will take (***13***, ***15***) amp plugs.
f. A dripping overflow means that the level of water in the cistern is too (***high***, ***low***).

3. Copy the diagram from page 135 into your notebooks, under the heading "How to wire a 13 amp plug". Add the correct colour for each wire.

4. Read the following electricity meter. Calculate how many units of electricity have been used.

5. Read the following gas meter. When you have calculated the number of cu ft of gas that have been used, change this figure into therms, assuming the calorific value is 500.

6. Design a poster that will show householders how they can avoid having burst pipes in winter.

7. Describe in your own words how you would:
a. mend a fuse; ***b.*** trace a gas leak; ***c.*** clear a blocked sink.

8. Choose a word from Column B to complete each sentence in Column A. Write out the completed sentences.

Column A	***Column B***
a. The supply of water to a house can be cut off by turning the	***fuse***
b. A . . . . . . is a safety device in electrical circuits.	***brown***
c. The live wire on an electrical appliance is coloured	***stop tap***
d. A . . . . should be used to unblock a sink.	***ball valve***
e. The neutral wire on an electrical appliance is coloured	***blue***
f. A . . . . regulates the water into a cistern.	***force pump***

9. Use your school and local libraries to find out about:
a. electricity power stations;
b. gas works;
c. reservoirs and filter beds.

10. Copy out this crossword and complete it.

Clues across

1. This supports electricity cables.
2. This needs changing if a tap starts to drip.
3. Used to record the amount of gas consumed.
4. May leak from a cistern.

Clues down

5. Gas is bought by the . . . .
6. You may need him if your pipes burst.
7. A type of fuse.

Part Four

Caring for a Family

CHAPTER 15

What is a family?

A family is a small group of people who, because of birth or choice, live together under one roof. The members of a family may differ one from another, in age, likes and dislikes, habits and attitudes, but each member of a family is important and should be loved and respected.

A family may consist of up to three generations of people. Let us consider the different age groups, the difficulties and problems that can arise, and how each group contributes to the happiness and well-being of the family unit.

A baby

A baby is usually a welcome addition to a family. While a baby is developing in the mother's womb, it is protected, nourished and kept warm. It is essential to the health of the developing baby, that the mother:

- ***a*** visits her doctor regularly;
- ***b*** attends ante-natal clinics, whenever possible, to monitor the progress of the baby;
- ***c*** drinks plenty of milk;
- ***d*** has vitamin and iron pills, which can be obtained at health centres and local clinics;
- ***e*** takes care not to over-exert herself;
- ***f*** avoids stretching, straining and lifting heavy objects;
- ***g*** does ***not*** smoke, take drugs or drink alcohol.

When a baby is born it needs much care and attention for the first few months of its life. A new-born baby is a helpless individual. It must be:

A new baby makes constant demands on the time, energies and patience of the other members of a family, but it can give happiness and love in return. A family will delight in watching the baby:

- ***a*** grow and develop;
- ***b*** respond to its surroundings;
- ***c*** recognize other members of the family;
- ***d*** learn to express itself;
- ***e*** learn to walk and talk;
- ***f*** explore its environment.

These stages in a baby's development can bring a family closer together. A family will unite in protecting, helping and encouraging during these early months.

A toddler

A baby quickly grows into a toddler with very definite ideas about life. The helpless member of the family has changed into an exploring, demanding individual, with a personality of his own. He is still too young to know the hazards that fire, electricity, water, poisons, sharp objects and traffic create, and care must be taken to guard against possible accidents in the home, garden and street.

A toddler should be encouraged to explore his environment. It is through play that the young child will learn, and he should be given the opportunity for:

- ***a*** sand, mud, plasticine, pastry and water play;
- ***b*** imaginative and creative play.

A toddler should be encouraged to become independent and to make decisions for himself. He will also make mistakes, but these are all part of the learning process. During these early years, a family should offer guidance in:

- ***a*** social habits;
- ***b*** attitudes;
- ***c*** good manners.

Honesty, generosity with possessions and loyalty to family and friends, should be encouraged.

Many toddlers attend play-groups, nursery schools, "Tufty clubs", etc. These enlarge a child's environment and introduce him to people outside his family group.

A young schoolchild

Going to school is the first step that many children take outside the protective care of their family.

The young child, by now, should be a self-possessed and confident individual. He should be encouraged to make new friends, play hard and work hard. He should have developed a definite sense of right and wrong, and though he will still need correction and guidance, he should be capable of making up his own mind. A family can help by including the young child in discussions and decisions so that he realizes his importance in the family unit.

The freedom to spend or save pocket money is useful training for adult life. A young child will need some guidance and encouragement, but he will gradually realize that money that is "budgeted" can be made to last longer. There is a thrill in saving up for a longed-for toy, and possessions obtained in this way are valued.

A young child should be encouraged to help in the home with simple jobs. In this way he will realize that belonging to a family brings its responsibilities, as well as its pleasures.

As a child grows, he will pass through various phases. There will be many occasions when he seems difficult, trying, awkward and aggressive, and many times when he seems sensible, practical and helpful. It is essential that a young child feels loved and important to his family, through bad phases as well as good ones. He should feel secure, and a family can help by providing a stable home-life.

An adolescent

Adolescence is the period during which a child develops into an adult. It can be a difficult, confusing time for a teenager, and for the members of his family. Adolescence brings changes: physical, emotional and mental.

These changes can create problems, and a family needs to be particularly understanding during this period. The physical changes experienced by an adolescent may cause him to feel tired, listless, awkward and self-conscious. The mental and emotional changes can create "moods" and a rebelliousness towards adults. These often show themselves in a defiant and critical attitude to parental authority. It is important that parents and other members of the family realize that these phases are normal, and part of the natural development of an individual from childhood to adulthood.

A family can help an adolescent by:

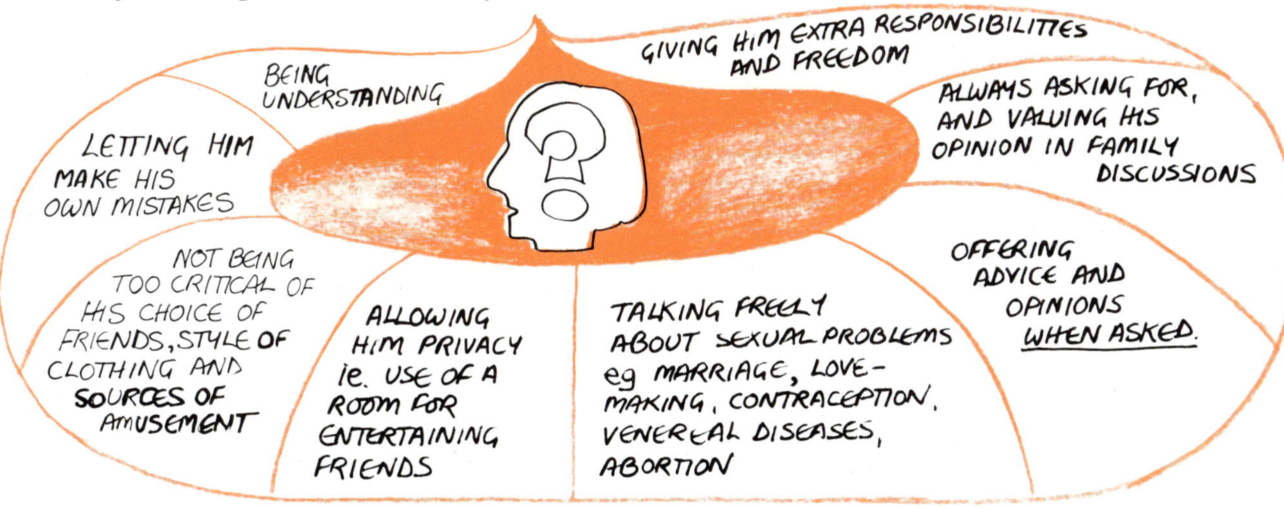

Parents

Parents provide shelter, food and clothing for their family. It is the responsibility of the father of the family to earn the money for these necessities. Many mothers choose to go out to work to supplement the family income but this is not a good thing when there are babies and very young children in the family. Can you think why not? When a mother has a full-time job outside the home, the family should try to help by sharing some of the household tasks.

Parents have the task of understanding the needs and problems of their family. This is not always easy, for as we have seen, each stage in a person's development brings its own particular problems and difficulties. Parents try to create a secure and happy home for their children. They try to support and encourage each member of the family, sympathize and console when necessary, be peacemakers in family quarrels, and be confidants and advisers. It is a formidable task.

Parents need to have some privacy, some time that they can call their own. They may wish to "go out together", pursue hobbies or just relax. Some parents join local groups and organizations, support Parent-Teacher gatherings, attend evening classes, go dancing or to the theatre, have an evening at the local pub or bingo hall.

Old people

When people grow old, they often find that because of poor health, a low income or loneliness, they cannot continue to live in their own home. Their family will have grown up, and may have married, moved to a new area and started their own families. In such a situation, elderly people may decide to live in one of these three ways ▶

It is not easy for old people to wrench themselves away from friends, a familiar neighbourhood, memories and treasured possessions. If elderly people choose to live with relatives, an attempt should be made to give them a feeling of independence. A separate room, where personal possessions and favourite pieces of furniture can surround them, will help to overcome the strangeness of their new home. An attempt should be made to keep in contact with old friends, as well as make new ones.

Elderly relatives living with a young family can create problems, but understanding, love and tolerance of each other's way of life, will help to smooth any difficulties. Young people should realize that older relatives want to remain:

- ***a*** active;
- ***b*** independent;
- ***c*** useful members of a family and of the community.

Old people who live in local authority homes, flats and bungalows, have the advantage of remaining in a familiar neighbourhood, often with their own friends. They can usually keep some of their favourite pieces of furniture, and so the wrench of leaving their own home is softened. Wardens are often provided in local authority homes and they are responsible for the welfare of the old people living there.

There is a wide range of services, voluntary organizations and clubs for elderly citizens. These include:

Men who are 65 years of age, and women who are 60 years of age, are eligible for a retirement pension, which is paid by the government.

A word about community centres

There are many community centres, colleges and schools, which open their doors to all age groups. Any and every member of a community is welcome to join in:

- ***a*** educational activities, e.g. day and evening classes, craft classes, training in the use of leisure time;
- ***b*** social activities, e.g. coffee bars, playgroups, whist drives, bingo-sessions, youth clubs;
- ***c*** leisure activities, e.g. swimming, football, darts, volley ball, table tennis, athletics.

These centres help to break down barriers, by integrating the different sections of a community. They aim to foster a community spirit and provide a real service for the families in their area.

Think and Do

1. Find out all you can about the voluntary organizations and services available for the old people in your particular area.

2. Arrange a visit to your local health centre and find out all you can on:

a. ante-natal care;

b. post-natal care;

c. welfare foods available to a mother and young baby.

3. Why is adolescence a difficult period? Say how a family can help a teenager through this stage in his development.

4. Find out where one would go and what one would do, to:

a. become a "home-help";

b. apply for an old person's bungalow or flat;

c. help with the "meals on wheels" service.

5. What do you think are the essentials of a good home?

6. Have a look around the toy shops in your area and make an illustrated list of toys that you think would encourage a toddler in imaginative and creative play.

7. In what ways can young schoolchildren help in the home, when both parents are working?

8. Draw a plan of your own family tree, showing the last three generations of people.

9. Make a list of the various activities you would expect to find in a good community centre.

10. Copy out this crossword and complete it.

Clues across

1. This person is in charge of the welfare of old people in local authority homes.
2. This type of leisure centre caters for all age groups.
3. Men are eligible for this when they are 65 years old.

Clues down

4. Children like to play with this.
5. A pregnant woman should not drink this.
6. A baby's first food.
7. A type of club for toddlers.

The health of a family

Healthy people enjoy life. They are active, interesting people, who are not always feeling ill and listless. We all have "off" days when we feel below par, but with a healthy attitude to life, we can soon shake off our depressions and feel fit again.

How can we help our families to be healthy? The answer is simple, by encouraging good habits. We should encourage each member of the family to:

- ***a*** sleep well;
- ***b*** eat well;
- ***c*** have plenty of fresh air and exercise;
- ***d*** be particular about personal cleanliness.

If these four golden rules are followed, then the result will be a happy, healthy, alert and active family.

The importance of sleep

Our bodies need to rest periodically. It is during these periods of rest (sleep) that bodily activities slow down, and damaged and worn cells are repaired and replaced.

The amount of sleep that each person needs will vary. Babies sleep for most of the day but adults find that around eight hours sleep is sufficient for their needs. Here is a chart of suggested sleep requirements for the various age groups in a family. Remember, though, that two people of the same age but doing different jobs of work, may require different periods of sleep, e.g. a person who has a sedentary job of work, perhaps sitting at a desk, will not be as physically tired at night, as a person who has expended a lot of energy during the daytime. This will affect the amount of sleep that each person requires.

It is a good idea for each member of the family to form regular bed-time habits. The odd "late" night will not hurt anybody, but do try to see that each person gets approximately his/her sleep requirements on most nights of the week.

The importance of a good diet

Our bodies need food to keep alive.

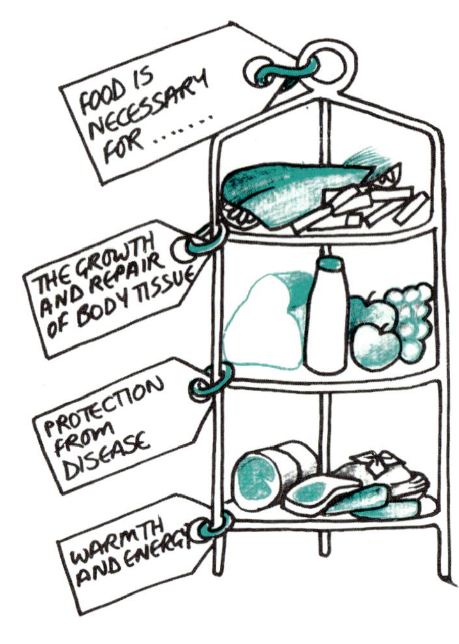

The main ***body-building*** foods are:

The main ***body-warming*** foods are:

The main ***energy-giving*** foods are:

The main ***body-protecting*** foods are:

When planning meals for the family, do try to see that foods from each of these groups are included. A well-balanced diet will help to keep your family healthy and fit. Try to encourage good meal-time habits. Meals should be eaten ***slowly*** and at ***regular intervals***. Hurried snacks may be convenient occasionally, but should not become a habit. Try to make meal times happy and relaxed when each member of the family can join in the conversation.

The importance of fresh air and exercise

Fresh air and exercise are good for our bodies.

Our bodies can manufacture ***Vitamin D*** from the action of sunlight on the skin. Vitamin D can be stored in our bodies. This means that sunbathing on a warm summer's day can help our bodies to keep healthy through the cold, winter months. (Remember to be careful when sunbathing. Too much sun can be harmful.)

All parts of our bodies can be stimulated by exercise.

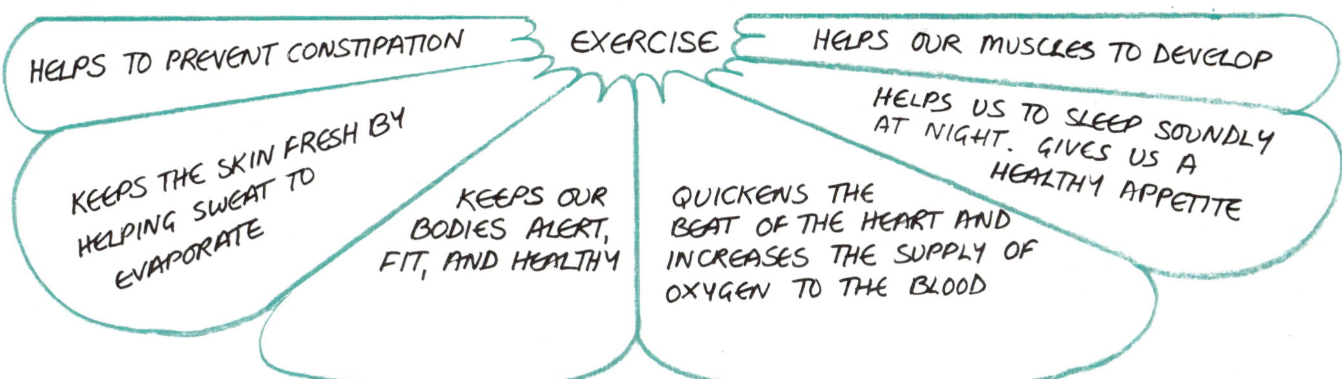

The importance of cleanliness

Good habits in personal hygiene should be encouraged in each member of the family, young and old. It should be an accepted rule that everybody:

- ***a*** has a good wash (teeth should be brushed as well) first thing in the morning and last thing at night;
- ***b*** washes his/her hands before ***each*** meal;
- ***c*** washes his/her hands after going to the lavatory.

Personal cleanliness is very important.

Skin has tiny holes or pores, all over its surface. The body gets rid of its waste products (grease, sweat) through the pores. It is important therefore that the pores are kept clean and open. Dirt and waste products, which are left on the skin, will clog the pores. This will:

- ***a*** prevent the sweat glands from working properly;
- ***b*** cause a stale, unpleasant smell;
- ***c*** encourage the growth of germs.

To keep the skin clean and healthy, wash frequently in hot, soapy water. A daily bath or shower is an excellent idea.

Always try to set an example in personal hygiene so that the other members of your family will want to copy you.

A word of warning

Never abuse your body. Do not be tempted to take pain-killing drugs frequently, unless your doctor has prescribed them. It is so easy to reach for a tablet when you have a headache, or feel irritable. It is much better to find out ***why*** you are having a headache and feeling irritable, and then try to deal with the cause of the problem. Could it be:

- ***a*** too many late nights;
- ***b*** not enough fresh air and exercise;
- ***c*** that you are not eating the right foods;
- ***d*** that your eyes need testing?

Do not be afraid to consult your doctor, when necessary. He or she is there to help you.

It is not clever to:

- ***a*** take drugs;
- ***b*** smoke cigarettes;
- ***c*** drink alcohol.

Find out the harm that you may be doing to yourself ***and*** to your family, if you abuse your body in these ways.

Protection from diseases

Children can be protected from some diseases by being ***vaccinated*** or ***inoculated***. There have been many advances in the field of preventive medicine during the past few decades. These vaccinations or inoculations are usually done at school. Do ask your doctor if you want advice.

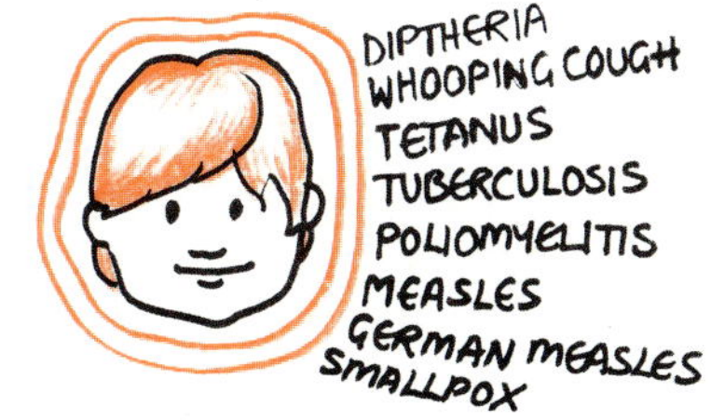

Preventing accidents in the home

Each year many people are injured or die as a result of accidents in the home. The majority of these accidents can be prevented. Let us consider the different kinds of hazards in a home and how it is possible to guard against them.

Injuries and deaths can result from:

How to guard against falls

1 Always see that staircases, halls and landings are well lit.

2 Do not leave unexpected objects on the floor where they can be tripped over.

3 Do not polish under loose mats.

4 See that the flexes from electrical appliances do not trail along the floor.

5 Check that worn floor coverings and mats are not in a dangerous state.

6 Wipe up spilt liquids and greases as soon as they occur.

7 Check that babies are securely fastened in their high chairs, push chairs, prams and "baby bouncers".
8 Use safety gates to protect toddlers from falling down staircases, and from running out of the garden.
9 Choose sensible footwear for yourself and your family. Some fashionable styles can be positively dangerous.
10 Do not climb on ordinary furniture. Always use a step-stool or stepladder. Can you think of any other precautions that will help to reduce the risk of falls in the home?

How to guard against burns and scalds

1 Always see that open fires, gas and electric fires are properly guarded.
2 Do not let young children play near a washing machine or cooker that is being used.
3 The handles of saucepans should be turned to the back or sides of a cooker. (Be very careful when cooking with hot fat.)
4 Run cold water into a bath, before turning on the hot tap.
5 Check that children cannot reach teapots, cups of tea and any hot dishes on a table.
6 Do not put mirrors, children's toys, clocks, letters and cards, etc. on a mantlepiece above a fire.
7 Always keep matches, lighter fuels and inflammable solutions away from young children.
8 Do not dry or air clothes near an unguarded fire.
9 Do not use an oil heater in a position where it might be knocked over. ***Never move an oil heater when it is lit.***
10 Buy non-inflammable or flame retardant clothing for your family, whenever possible. This is especially important for children's nightwear.
11 ***Never look for a gas leak with a naked flame.***
12 Always be wary of fireworks. Store them safely and use them sensibly.
13 Try to teach young children which household items are inflammable, e.g. aerosol canisters.
14 If you are a smoker always use an ash tray. ***Never smoke in bed.***
Can you think of any other precautions that will reduce the risk of burns and scalds in the home?

How to guard against poisoning

1 Check that town gas appliances are serviced regularly. Do not let children play with gas taps or gas meters.

2 If the gas supply is cut, turn off all gas taps immediately. When the gas supply comes on, check that all pilot lights are lit.

3 Always ensure that there is adequate ventilation in rooms that have a gas appliance. This is especially important if water is heated by a gas geyser in a bathroom.

4 Keep all medicines in a special cabinet. This should be locked if there are young children in a family.

5 Never store cleaning fluids or chemicals in empty soft drink bottles. Always keep bleaches and disinfectants away from young children.

6 Always teach children not to eat things that they may find in a garden, e.g. berries, laburnum seeds, fungi.

7 Keep weedkillers and all garden chemicals in a locked cupboard in the garage or garden shed.

Can you think of any other precautions that will reduce the risk of poisoning in the home?

How to guard against suffocation

1 Do not let young babies sleep on a pillow.

2 ***Never let a child play with a plastic bag.***

3 Do not leave a baby to feed itself, by propping a bottle in its mouth.

4 Always check that a baby has "brought up wind" before putting it down to sleep.

5 A baby or young child should not sleep in the same bed as its parents, because of the danger of over-laying.

6 Do not leave plastic-backed bibs on, after a baby has been fed.

7 Use a safety net to prevent family pets from sleeping on prams, pushchairs and cots.

8 See that old, airtight appliances, e.g. refrigerators, are removed by the local authorities. If this cannot be done immediately, take off any doors that have catches or locks.

Try to think of other precautions that will reduce the risk of suffocation in the home.

How to guard against drowning

1 Garden ponds should be covered or fenced around, if there are young children about.
2 Encourage all members of your family to learn to swim, the younger the better.
3 Encourage all members of your family to learn to life-save, and make sure that they know how to give artificial respiration in an emergency.
4 Young children should be taught the dangers of rivers, ponds, lakes, reservoirs, the sea, wells, mine shafts and gravel pits.
Can you think of any other precautions that will reduce the risk of drowning?

Other hazards in the home

Care should be taken when handling electrical equipment. All electrical appliances should be serviced regularly. Broken plugs and frayed flexes should be replaced immediately. Always check that the correct rating of fuse is used in plugs and fuse boxes, and only use one electrical appliance for each power socket. ***Never take portable electrical equipment into a bathroom.***

Signs of safety

Learn to recognize signs. They can be found on appliances that have passed safety tests and are approved by Consumer Protection bodies. The ones shown here are the "kitemark" for many goods and, below that, those for electrical, oil or gas appliances respectively.

Fire

If, despite all your precautions, a fire breaks out in your home, ***keep calm***.
1 See that every member of the family leaves the building by the quickest route. Do not let anybody stop to collect his or her "treasures".
2 Call the fire brigade.
3 While waiting for the fire brigade, try to reduce draughts that could fan the fire, by closing all doors and windows.

BS 5258

Be prepared

In an emergency, you will have to think quickly and clearly. Keep a list of useful telephone numbers in a handy place (by the telephone?), e.g.

Doctor	......
Dentist	......
Plumber	......
Electrician	......
Gas Board	......
Fire, Police, Ambulance	999

If you do not have a telephone, keep some coins handy too. You may need them if you use a call box.

Think and Do

1. Copy this diagram into your notebook, making it larger if you can. Write a suitable sentence in each of the boxes.

2. Suggest ways that the following people can get adequate exercise.

a. a shorthand typist;
b. a young schoolgirl;
c. a long-distance lorry driver;
d. a middle-aged woman recovering from influenza.

3. Design a poster that will make people more aware of accident prevention in the home.

4. Copy the diagram from the bottom of page 149 into your notebook under the heading "Care of the skin". Describe why it is important to keep the skin clean.

5. Visit your local and school libraries and find out all you can on each of the following:

a. the harmful effects of smoking;
b. recent advances in preventive medicine;
c. habit-forming drugs.

6. In your notebook, draw diagrams of the Consumer Protection safety marks (see page 154). Label each sign clearly.

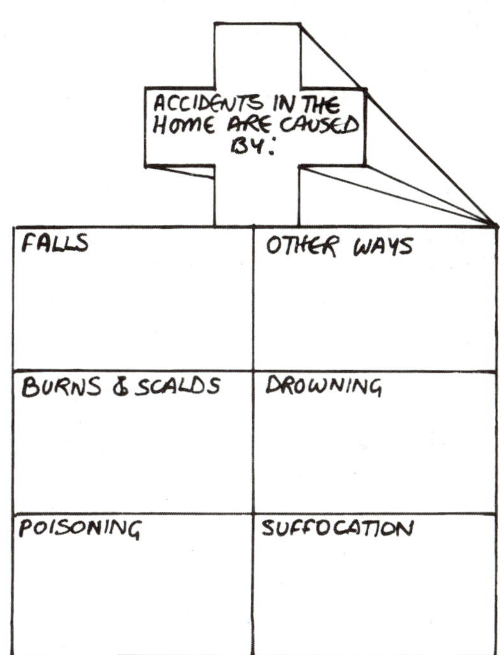

7. Why is it important to have a balanced diet? Suggest a suitable meal for each of the following:

a. lunch for two old-age pensioners on a cold, winter's day;

b. high tea for Dad and two teenagers who have been watching a football match;

c. a picnic meal for the family on a day's hike.

8. In the picture below there are many hazards to safety. List them in your notebook.

9. Are the following sentences ***true*** or ***false***?

a. A teenager should have about ten hours of sleep a night.

b. Milk and cheese are good body-building foods.

c. Vitamin C can be manufactured in the body by the action of sunlight on the skin.

d. Exercise quickens the beat of the heart and increases the supply of oxygen to the blood.

e. Children can be vaccinated against smallpox while at school.

f. Consumer Protection bodies label approved household appliances with safety signs.

10. Copy out this crossword and complete it.

Clues across

1. A rest period for the body.
2. This makes nails neat and tidy.
3. A good energy-giving food.

Clues down

4. This cleanses the body thoroughly.
5. Keeps the body fit and active.
6. A hole in the skin.

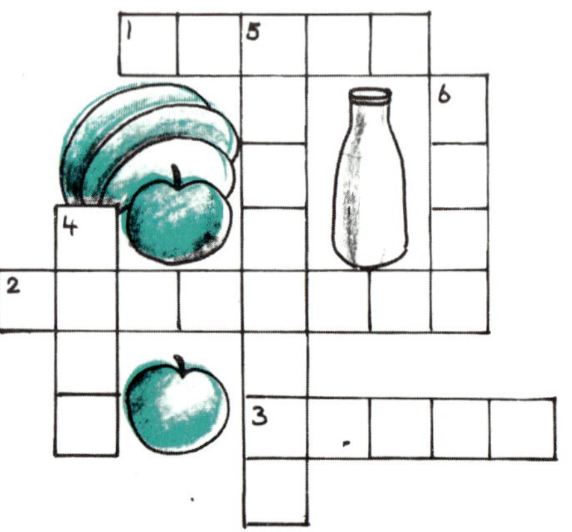